I0752497

New Brunswick and the Civil War

The Brunswick Boys in the Great Rebellion

Joanne Hamilton Rajoppi

Published by The History Press
Charleston, SC 29403
www.historypress.net

Cover images: Long Branch Military Band. *Author's collection, New Brunswick Free Public Library Postcard Collection*; the Soldiers and Sailors' monument. *New Brunswick Free Public Library Postcard Collection*; the New Jersey Rubber Shoe Company. *From* History of Union and Middlesex Counties, New Jersey.

First published 2013

ISBN 978-1-5402-2220-6

Library of Congress CIP data applied for.

Notice: The information in this book is true and complete to the best of our knowledge. It is offered without guarantee on the part of the author or The History Press. The author and The History Press disclaim all liability in connection with the use of this book.

To the Hamiltons and to all those who served.

Contents

PREFACE

I see that the boys are leaving Brunswick yet to go in the Army and I...would not be satisfied if I were home.
–August 22, 1861, camp near Seminary, Virginia

One of the great legacies we can pass to our families is a record of our lives—a testament to the accomplishments, joys, tragedies and failures. Such a gift came to me many years ago in the form of my great-grandfather's letters. Written to his mother in New Brunswick, New Jersey, while he served in the Civil War, his letters number more than eighty and chronicle his life as a soldier, the lives of his hometown friends who went with him and the families they all left behind.

These treasured and worn letters, copied by a member of my great-grandfather's immediate family (most likely one of his daughters), were then bound in a ledger book and passed on to my great-aunt, the late Jennie Hamilton Bolshaw of Hasbrouck Heights, New Jersey.

The book then started its own unique journey. Jennie passed the book to her nephew, my uncle, the late John Herbert Hamilton of Bernardsville, New Jersey, who subsequently bequeathed it to his daughter, Gail Hamilton Willoughby Gaugler of Texas. Gail reproduced the letters in the worn and deteriorating ledger and, in turn, made copies for her sons, Christopher and Glenn, as well as my mother, Mildred Hamilton Rajoppi; my sister, Carol; and myself. We each received a copy of the book in December 1972, a little more than one hundred years after they were written.

When I first saw the letters, I was curious, but I did little more than glance at the difficult-to-read nineteenth-century handwriting, deciphering at first those iconic words that jumped from the pages like "Antietam" and "Gettysburg." When I read the letters again years later, however, I was amazed by their breadth and universality. The letters follow my great-grandfather, John P. Hamilton, through three years of war, the deaths of two family members, the loss of friends and the experiences of forming lifelong bonds.

There were seven hundred men and boys from New Brunswick who joined John in wearing the Union blue. He knew many of them from the rubber factory where he worked; others, like Charlie Banks, a porter in a store, and Jule Meyers, a boatman, were acquaintances from town. The "Boys" were seventeen- and eighteen-year-olds for the most part, although many of their older or younger brothers joined as well for what they believed would be a three-month frolic to crush the "Rebels." Some, lured by the prospect of better wages, signed on to meet otherwise unattainable dreams, while others were attracted by the adventure of simply traveling beyond their hometown.

The Hamilton family was in the thick of it. Brothers Aleck, nineteen, the oldest, and James, sixteen, the youngest, joined their middle brother, John, seventeen. Even their father, Alexander, then forty-eight, traveled to Pennsylvania to join Company D, Fifty-seventh Pennsylvania Regiment Volunteers. John's father, my great-great-grandfather, was the oldest man in his company. Called "Elder" by his comrades, he joined a select group of men who, while perhaps considered beyond their prime, served as "privates" in the army.

John's letters, which span his enlistment from June 1861 to June 1864, when he was discharged, convey everyday struggles to survive while seeking the comfort of fellowship and connection to home. Reflecting the culture of his time, his letters portray the larger drama of living and fighting in a war.

Letters, both written and received, were the primary way to communicate with those at home, to let them know of a soldier's safety, while learning what was happening with dear family and friends left behind. While the telegraph was in wide use by the 1850s, it was more widely used by the government to dispatch orders. Letters, on the other hand, were the soldiers' method of communication, and they were anticipated and expected. Many wrote home daily, or at least several times per week. When late, there was disappointment and worry for both sender and receiver.

One can only infer what John's mother and sister wrote from his responses. Sadly, to my knowledge, only his letters were saved and passed down. Although it seems reasonable to speculate that John may have handed over the treasured letters of his mother to one of the Brunswick Boys on furlough to return to his mother's safekeeping, or that perhaps he even lost them as they were kept in his knapsack, there is no record of her letters.

Perhaps most upsetting was the "cliffhanger" presented to me as John's enlistment came to an end. Having lost family and friends, he wrote to his mother, who had not responded in more than two months to his letters. Her last communication informed him of her own illness and her hopes of seeing him soon. His letters end at his discharge and do not tell us what awaited him when he returned to New Brunswick.

Disappointed and curious as to what happened upon his return, I shadowed John's homecoming through my own yearlong odyssey spent in local and university libraries, culling old city directories, archives and dusty family albums, visiting historical societies and searching graveyards for a life story. My search took me from journals to battlefields, to twisting avenues and dead ends while discovering these Boys who had suddenly been turned into men by the deprivation and horror of war. Happily, I also learned how they went forward to create productive lives when the war ended. At times, my research dead-ended due to lost, destroyed or tattered records, especially for John's sister Susan. I can only speculate on her tragic end.

I spent hours bent over historic journals and old newspapers to discover direct descendants of Alexander and Mary Ann Hamilton, who are alive today. Besides my sister, Carol, and my cousin, Gail, I found two other Hamilton cousins, Arlene and Jean Bolshaw, and I suspect that there are many more I can anticipate meeting in the future when we discover one another. The Internet assisted in my search and provided hints and teasers that led me to places like Eel, Indiana; Detroit, Michigan; Seattle, Washington; and Los Angeles, California, where I would never have thought to investigate but struck gold when I did.

There were endless hours, too, spent on the Internet looking for connections between the Hamilton family members. There were numerous phone calls and letters to historians and antiquarians whose collections might house photographs of the Brunswick Boys.

On at least two occasions, John used the word "n*****" in his letters home. Derived from the Spanish word *negro* (for black) in the seventeenth century, the word has a long and offensive connotation. Today, it remains one of the most pejorative words in the English language, and yet to eliminate it from John's two letters would not be true to the cultural and historic context of his time. I include it in its abbreviated form with apologies for any offense to readers.

I formatted John's letters into chronological groups and precede each group of letters with a chapter to correlate the life of war with the life at home. In transcribing John's letters, I have taken the liberty of adding punctuation, which he did not seem to appreciate, and formatted the letters into paragraphs. Where necessary, I corrected spelling to convey a word or correctly spell a proper name; otherwise, all of the spellings are John's. I also have placed superscript numbers next to terms not in current use with an explanation as to their meaning. Although not complete, I have included a large sample of John's letters.

In addition, many Civil War battles are known by two widely used names; often the North named battles for bodies of water or other natural features, while the Confederates used the name of the nearest town or man-made landmark. I employ the designation of two names where applicable for battles, with the Federal name appearing first followed by the Confederate name.

Although I suspect more is known about many of the other individual Brunswick Boys through contemporary accounts and perhaps other existing letters passed down through their descendants of the era, I had to end my investigation at a point where I felt I could tell their story. I sincerely hope that readers who may have information on any of the Boys' family histories, photographs, letters and so forth will write to me in care of the publisher so that I might include that important additional information for later editions.

My hope, too, is that readers find my great-grandfather's letters as alive today as when he wrote them—letters from a New Brunswick Boy who did his duty like so many others before and after him with little complaint. His letters are about the Boys who came with him to serve and their lives. John calls his fellow soldiers from home the "Brunswick Boys," and so do I. God bless them all!

ACKNOWLEDGEMENTS

Imagine my delight during my research when I discovered librarians and government officials who were not only Civil War aficionados but reenactors as well, like New Brunswick Library director Dr. Robert Belvin and New Brunswick city clerk Dan Torrisi. Their input and generosity in sharing their knowledge of a soldier's life was invaluable. Grateful thanks also to the staff at the former New Jersey Division of Archives and Records Management; New Jersey Psychiatric Hospital; Special Collections at Rutgers University; Detroit City Library; Long Branch Library; Monmouth County Historical Society; New Brunswick City Library; the Township of Ocean Historical Museum; and Union County Historical Society for their energetic and knowledgeable assistance.

A special acknowledgement goes to my colleagues who serve as New Jersey constitutional officers, especially Essex County surrogate Theodore H. Stephens II, Monmouth County clerk Claire French and Surrogate Rosemarie Peters, Middlesex County clerk Elaine Flynn and Bergen County surrogate Michael R. Dressler. Their excellent records were a resource in locating many Hamilton relatives and reunited me with two "lost" Hamilton cousins.

Librarians and historians are truly a writer's best friends. To Bob McAvoy, who helped me search for my great-great-grandfather's grave, your optimism gave me hope that we will find it someday. Many thanks to my friend Todd Jordan for his love of military history and skill at explaining it to me. Last, but not least, my gratitude to Gary Szelc, friend and fellow writer, who painstakingly read this manuscript more than once and provided a number of insights into the military, historic and chronological aspects of the mid- to late nineteenth century.

Chapter 1
CALL TO ARMS

I am well and enlisted and sworn into the service.
—June 26, 1861, Camp Olden, Trenton, New Jersey

Soon after those fateful shots rang out at Fort Sumter, South Carolina, signaling the start of the Civil War in April 1861, President Abraham Lincoln called on all "able-bodied" men to serve their country.

Despite the political reality of New Jersey voting for Stephen A. Douglas in the presidential election of 1860 and acting, in many respects, like a "border state," the Garden State did not lack patriotic fervor. There were speeches, official resolutions and parades. Everyone waved flags, and most shared the belief that the North would trample the South in a few weeks, certainly no later than the Fourth of July. Hastily, regiments were formed throughout the North, and men tripped over one another to enlist. There was the prospect of steady wages and adventure to boot.

Out of the ten thousand people who inhabited New Brunswick, a booming industrial town located on the transport hub of the Delaware and Raritan Canal, more than seven hundred boys and men joined the Union effort, quickly filling the New Brunswick Regiment, one of the four regiments President Abraham Lincoln called for in his quota for the state.

John P. Hamilton of New Brunswick had just turned eighteen in 1861 and was caught in the race to enlist. Gray-eyed with dark hair and a fair complexion, John was tall for the time, measuring five feet, seven inches. Working at Meyer Rubber Factory with his father, Alexander, forty-eight,

The Soldiers and Sailors' monument in New Brunswick is dedicated to the city men who served in the Civil War. *New Brunswick Free Public Library Postcard Collection.*

and his brother, James, sixteen, he longed for the excitement that filled the news and the clear, clean air away from the hot machinery and toxic smells that he experienced as a machinist for eleven hours a day making rubber soles for shoes.

The Hamilton family had moved to New Brunswick from Lynn, Massachusetts, the women's shoe capital of the world, a few years earlier. For decades, Lynn was a major center for shoe manufacturing, all made by hand until the introduction of the sewing machine in about 1851.

As early as 1840, Alexander Hamilton; his wife, Mary Ann; and their daughter, Mary Jane, lived in Lynn. Alexander was exceptionally tall for the time, measuring six feet, two inches. With a light complexion, gray eyes and dark hair, he must have made a striking figure walking the streets of Lynn. Shortly after Mary Jane was born in 1838 in Massachusetts, Alexander Jr. ("Aleck") made his entry into the world in 1842 in New Hampshire, followed by John in 1844 and James in 1845, both born in Vermont; Frances P., who likely died shortly after her birth in March 1849; Susan later that year; and finally, Alice in 1852, the last three born in Massachusetts.

Although there was no recorded reason for Alexander Sr.'s moves among the states of Massachusetts, New Hampshire, Vermont and then back to Massachusetts in the twelve-year span of his children's births, the New England states were the national center for shoemaking throughout the nineteenth century, with Massachusetts supplying 50 percent of the nation's total shoemaking production. Preindustrial shoemaking was focused on domestic production in families, so it would not be unusual for shoemaking families to move at will. Their homes were literally their factories in the handmade shoe process.

While Alexander, an expert shoe laster (or cordwainer, as it was known), may have been lured to New Brunswick by the newly rebuilt Meyer Rubber Company, it is more likely that the Panic of 1857, an economic depression when prices plummeted and businesses responded by slashing wages, led Alexander and his family to leave Lynn.

In some Lynn shops, wages were cut to as little as fifty cents per day due to the economic downturn. It was impossible to provide for his growing family on such meager wages. More money could be made in New Jersey, and the Meyer Rubber Factory was looking for skilled shoemakers. Alexander Sr. had a growing family to support.

Oldest son Aleck did not make the move to New Jersey with the family. In 1858, at age sixteen, Aleck was old enough to be on his own; he was

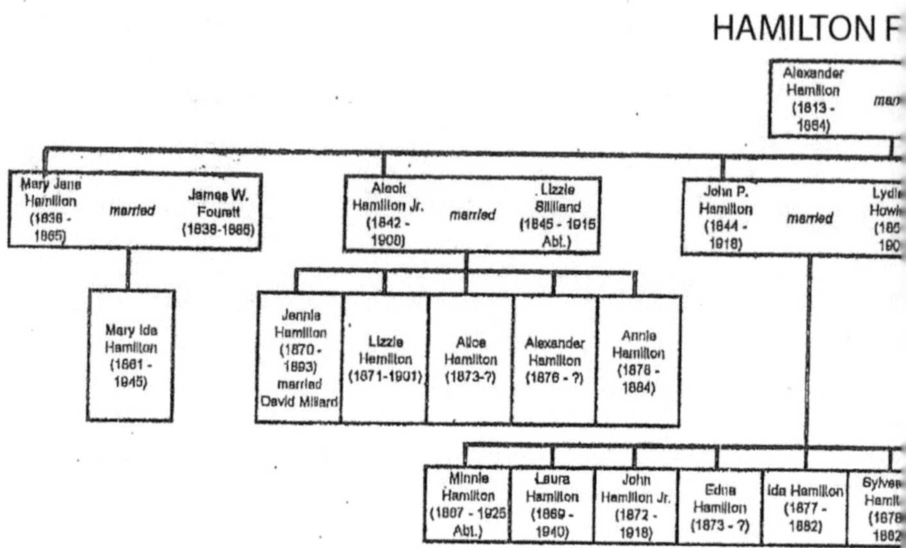

more adapt at carpentry than shoemaking, and skilled cabinetmakers were in demand. Aleck also had a streak of wanderlust that would reappear many times in his life. Traveling to Indiana, he apprenticed himself to a master journeyman there.

Joining the influx of German and Irish immigrants to New Brunswick, the Hamilton family found work at the New Jersey Rubber Company, one of three rubber companies headquartered in the city. Father Alexander and son John made shoes; later, James joined them at the company, working in the store. Two hundred men and women worked at Meyer and turned out three thousand pairs of boots and shoes each year at a value of $500,000, a significant sum at the time, worth about $10 million today.

Located on Washington Street near Peace, the New Jersey Rubber Company also employed John's older sister, Mary Jane, as a weaver until her marriage to James Fouratt. Working-class women generally worked until they married. As a woman, Mary Jane earned much less than her brothers and father but toiled the same number of hours doing tedious work. When Mary Jane married on January 1, 1861, at age twenty-three, she terminated her employment to become a full-time housekeeper, wife and, soon thereafter, mother.

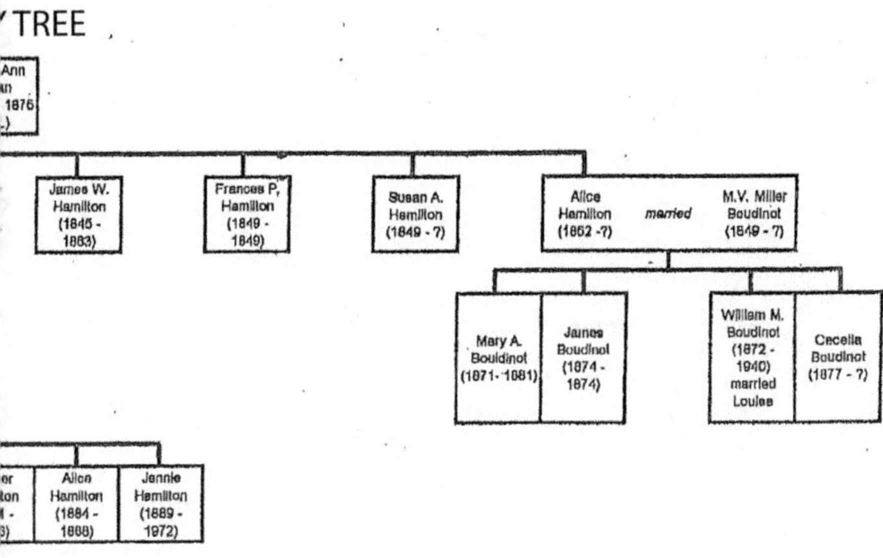

The New Jersey Rubber Shoe Company in New Brunswick was a successor to Meyer Rubber Company, where the Hamilton men worked. *From* History of Union and Middlesex Counties, New Jersey, with Illustrations, *edited by W. Woodford Clayton, 1882.*

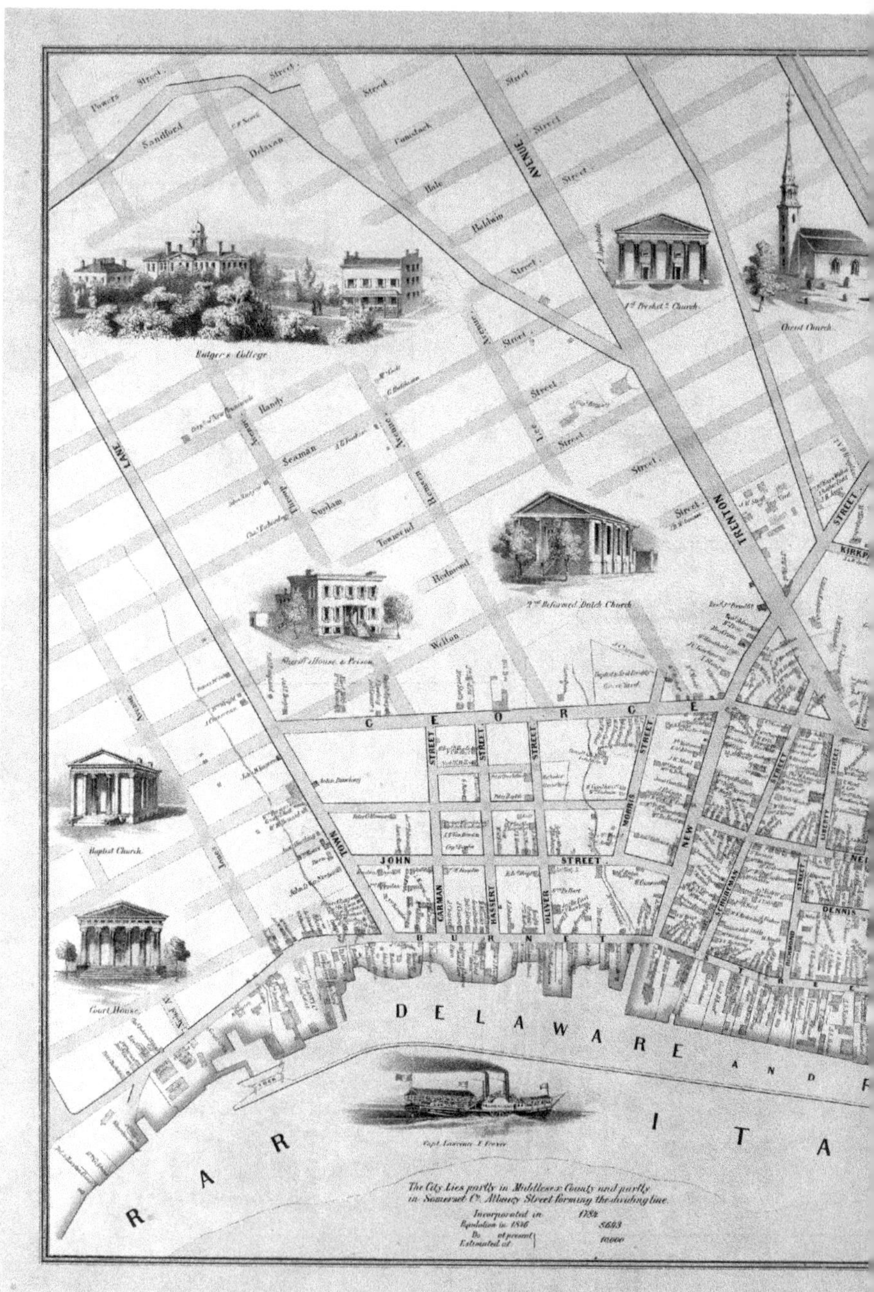

This 1850 New Brunswick map depicts the Delaware and Raritan Canal and churches in the city. *Rutgers Special Collections.*

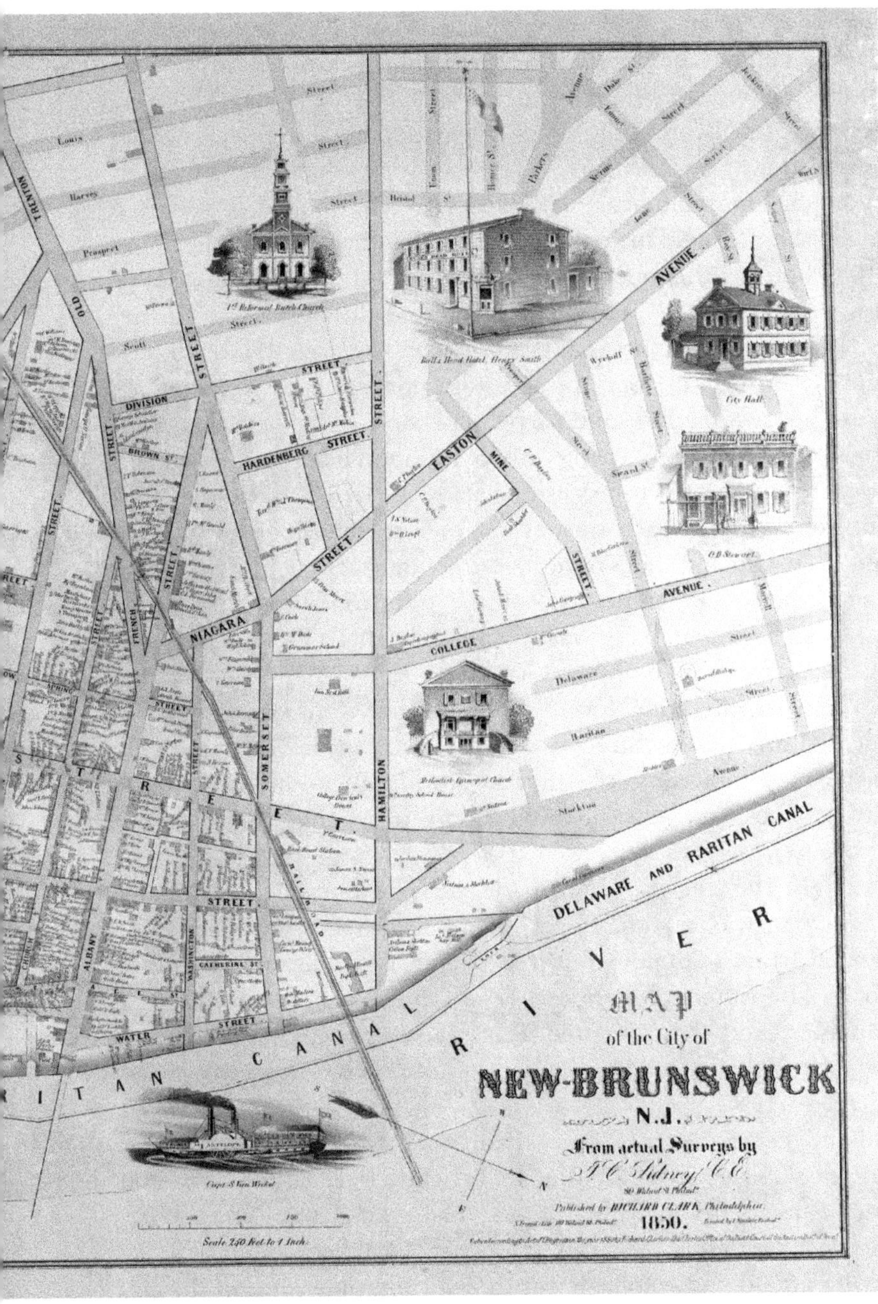
MAP
of the City of
NEW-BRUNSWICK
N.J.
From actual Surveys by
J. C. Sidney C. E.
Published by RICHARD CLARK Philadelphia.
1850.
DELAWARE AND RARITAN CANAL
RIVER
CANAL
EASTON AVENUE
COLLEGE AVENUE
NIAGARA STREET
HAMILTON
SOMERSET
HARDENBERG STREET
DIVISION STREET
BROWN ST.
FRENCH
OLD TRENTON
ALBANY
WASHINGTON
CATHERINE ST.
WATER STREET
CHURCH
MINE STREET
Delaware
Raritan
City Hall
Scale 250 Feet to 1 Inch.

Christopher Meyer, owner and entrepreneur of the New Jersey Rubber Company, also operated a large factory, the New Jersey Rubber Shoe Company, situated along side the Lawrence Brook in what is now Milltown, just to the west of New Brunswick proper. The company's original buildings had been destroyed by two earlier fires. When they were rebuilt, there were six new stand-alone factory buildings—separated sufficiently, it was hoped, as a precaution against a fire breaking out in any one building and spreading.

The building housing the machinery was located on the opposite side of the brook away from the shoemaking building and the ovens as a further precaution. Grinding mills were housed in a separate brick building. The largest structure was the four-story frame building for the actual shoemaking; the factory also housed machine and carpenter shops.

The business of turning rubber into usable products like shoes was a hot, smelly, tedious, machine-driven process. Alexander Hamilton, in one short decade, went from crafting leather shoes in a piecemeal fashion by hand in Massachusetts to producing shoes almost entirely by machine in New Jersey. He, like many others, was at the cusp of the Industrial Revolution. The one constant was that shoemaking was still a family affair: fathers, sons and daughters were all employed in the factory.

Mr. Meyer also operated the Novelty Hard Rubber Company beginning in 1853. Located on Neilson Street above the railroad bridge, it was the country's largest manufacturer of rubber buttons. In addition, it made smoking pipes, canes and knitting pins. Some of young John's friends worked at Novelty.

Industry was also thriving elsewhere in the city. The Janeway & Company, a wallpaper factory, was established in 1844 on Water Street facing the Delaware and Raritan Canal. A few years later, a candle manufacturer located nearby. The Empire Machine Works, which manufactured textile knitting machines, and Consolidated Fruit Jar Company, which made metal screw tops with liners for glass jars, established themselves a few years later.

The gem and centerpiece of New Brunswick was Queen's College, renamed Rutgers College in 1825 after its benefactor, Revolutionary War colonel Henry Rutgers (today, it is Rutgers, The State University of New Jersey). One of the oldest institutions of higher learning in America, the young men who attended the college were a common sight around the city, shopping, eating at local restaurants and rowing on the canal.

The school's oldest building, Old Queens, was built between 1809 and 1825, and its premier Federal architecture was a distinctive landmark in

Rutgers College, one of the oldest institutions of higher learning in America at the time, was the gem of New Brunswick. *New Brunswick Free Public Library Postcard Collection.*

the city. The block surrounding it, known as Old Queens Campus, was close to the heart of the city, bound by Somerset Street to the east, George Street to the north, College Avenue to the south and Hamilton Street to the west.

Another important institute of learning, the New Brunswick Theological Seminary, a professional and graduate school founded to educate ministers for the Reformed Church of America, shared facilities with Rutgers up until 1856, when it outgrew its location and moved half a mile away.

There were also many shops, churches, two newspapers, schools, German cultural clubs and benevolent or charitable societies throughout the city. There were opportunities to boat on the canal, stroll along the streets with friends and ice-skate in the winter on the ponds. Through his work and family, John had many friends and acquaintances throughout the city and developed lasting friendships.

When the call for men to join the Union cause came to New Brunswick, John discussed going to war with his family: his father, his mother, younger brother James and his married sister, Mary Jane. His little sisters—Susan, twelve, and Alice, nine—probably listened with rapt attention. John knew that his father longed to put together a sufficient amount of money to buy a small farm, a piece of land he could own where he could grow his own food away from the smell and fumes of the rubber factory.

John probably thought that he could earn more money by enlisting than working long hours at the factory. Yet both his father and mother must have been reluctant to have their middle son go to war and most likely provided some stern and practical advice, hoping that he would stay in New Brunswick despite the enthusiasm of his sixteen-year-old brother, James, who was disappointed that his parents would not allow him to join John. Oldest son Aleck, far away in Indiana, had already enlisted in April. Wasn't one son in the war enough of a contribution to the cause?

The coming war was all that John's friends—many of whom worked at the Meyer Rubber Company, like Jim Furlong and John Tyler Lewis—could talk about, but by the time John decided to enlist, the two Brunswick companies had been filled.

In early June 1861, John along with best friend Jim Furlong enlisted and traveled to Trenton. When they reached Camp Olden in Trenton, the only company open to them was Company K, First New Jersey Regiment. The company had been organized in Hoboken, a bustling town in northeast New Jersey along the Hudson River, and more than two-thirds of the fifty-five men in the company were Dutch or German, with names like Diehl, Furchenicht, Getterman, Krauss, Lindermann, Schellenberg, Schmidt, Vroom and Vanduzen.

It was certainly a culture shock to young John Hamilton to be thrown in with men who spoke a language he didn't understand and who, for the most part, were very recent immigrants to America. Many of the Germans in New Brunswick were skilled, experienced craftspeople with tightly knit social organizations, and it is doubtful that John and his English-speaking friends interacted with them.

Still, John was personally knowledgeable about those who came from other countries. Best friend Jim Furlong had emigrated from Ireland with his father, and John's own mother, Mary Ann Ryan, was born in Halifax, Nova Scotia. Their lilting voices, though, were far different from the guttural sounds emanating from his new comrades, as was their love for "stinking" cheese. Still, he found his fellow enlistees "clean men," as he told his mother in one letter, and like many young men, he adapted so well that he could understand their language after time.

Despite having been born in Vermont and then moving with his family first to Massachusetts and then to New Jersey, John was not well traveled. Many people at that time rarely traveled more than fifty miles from their home over a lifetime. So, after arriving in Washington, D.C., by convoy train a few days after his enlistment, John acted like an excited tourist rather than a soldier going to war as he admired the view of the city and the construction of the Capitol Building. "The capitol is not finished yet," he explained to his mother, adding with awe, "It is all built of marble."

John's connection to home remained strong. When he saw another Brunswick lad, Charlie Banks, formerly a porter in a New Brunswick shop, he wrote to his mother asking her to tell Jane Gelager, a friend of the two boys, of Charlie's good health. "He looks well, only a little sun burned. He says he likes it [the Volunteers] first rate."

Within the month, John would be "at war." He was given orders to shoot "anything that moves," including a dog, and escaped the bloodshed of the First Battle of Bull Run, living "like a King" and eating well. It was a short respite; the reality of the war was about to begin for him.

Camp Olden, Trenton, New Jersey
June 26th 1861

Dear Mother,

I write you a few lines to let you know that I am well and enlisted and sworn into the service. The two Brunswick Companys were full and the only Company I could get into was a Dutch company from Hoboken, Co. K.

Their is only one man in the company that is not Dutch. They appear to be a clean set of men and I guess I will get along with them very well. Jim Furlong is with me so their is 3 men in the company that can understand each other.

We leave for Washington on the 28th. You may hear from me again before we go. When you write to Aleck tell him where I am and to write to me as soon as he gets where he can get an answer.

Love to all,

From your afectionate son,
John

Camp Montgomery near Washington
June 30th 1861

Dear Mother,

I write you a few lines to let you know where I am and how I am getting along. We left Trenton on Friday morning at about half past 7 o'clock. On the cars[1] before we got to Baltimore we got orders to load our rifles with ball and powder. The musket-balls were too large for our rifles so we had to cut them down small with our knifes. We got there at about 9 o'clock in the evening. We expected the mob would attack us and we hoped they would so we could give them a lesson for what they had done before.[2]

I think we could have cleaned Baltimore out for we were 3 Regiments and over a thousand men to each and all the mens' guns were loaded and caped. They insulted us by cheering for Jeff Davis and groaning for Lincoln but our officers would not let us touch them without they attacked us. So we had to let them alone and it went against the grain, I can tell you.

From our camp we had a fine view of Washington. It is a large place. The capitol is not finished yet. It is all built of marble. I was in the City this morning. I was through the Capitol and the Presidents Garden.

We saw a lot of the Brunswick Boys that are out here in the 3 months regiment. Tell Jane Gelager I saw Charlie Banks and he looks well only a little sun burnt. He says he likes it first rate.

No more at present.

From your afectionate son,
John

1. "Cars" were railroad cars and the main transportation for Union soldiers over long distances throughout the war.
2. Pro-secessionist rioters had attacked Union troops traveling through Baltimore on April 15–20, 1861.

Washington
July the 24th 1861

Dear Mother,

I suppose you feel very anxious to hear from me by this time and having an opportunity you shall know what I have been doing since I wrote you last. 15 minutes after I mailed the last letter I wrote you we got orders to march South and were on the road in half an hour. In about another half hour we heard heavy firing in front of us and not long after we got news that the army were fighting at Bull Run.[1]

Just before dark we commenced to meet the wounded coming past in ambulances. It was the first wounded I had saw and it was hard sight—we got there a little to late to get in the fight. They were bringing the last of the wounded off the field. When we got there we formed a line and lay on our arms until all the Army had retreated past us and the next morning we came on towards Washington covering the retreat and bringing all the wounded ambulance wagons and anything that we could not bring along, we burned.

We arrived here on Monday morning at about 10 o'clock after marching about 60 miles without stopping longer than 10 minutes at a time to rest. Some of the boys found several things on the battle field. Jule Myers found a carbine and some found pistols, bowie knifes, etcetera.

I think that if we had got up there in time we would have whipped the Rebs for their were over 3000 of us and that is a good many, but it is no use talking now. We are in camp now near the Georgetown Canal and can go in swimming and it is a good place to wash our cloths.

No more at present.

From your afectionate son,
John

1. July 21, 1862, the day the Battle of Bull Run/First Manassas took place.

Chapter 2
Hamilton Men at War

Since I wrote...I have saw Aleck. I knew him as soon as I saw him.
–September 16, 1861, Camp Seminary, Virginia

Within a few months of John's enlistment, his father, Alexander Hamilton, traveled to Pennsylvania, where he hoped to buy property, probably a farm, to which the family could move, far away from the congestion of the city. We can only speculate that the move to Pennsylvania was a prelude for him to claim land upon his return from the army. He hoped to pay for the property with the money he earned during his military service.

The general consensus at the start of the war was that it would be over quickly, no more than a few months at the most. The perceived short period and the lure of increased pay over factory wages enticed men like Alexander Hamilton, who dreamed of homeownership. Enlisting and serving could mean the difference between renting and owning a home for some.

The Hamilton patriarch, his son wrote to his mother in March 1862, "has been talking to me about that place he picked out in Pennsylvania and...I think we had better buy it and then we will have a home of our own."

The Hamilton family did not own property either in New Jersey or Massachusetts, renting their home in New Brunswick, possibly from the factory. Historically, urban workers like the Hamiltons had lower homeownership rates than those living, for example, in farm areas. Homeownership was closely tied to aspirations for stability and well-being. According to social scientists Peter H. Rossi and Anne B. Shlay, "Owning

A view of Codwise Avenue, now Joyce Kilmer Avenue, in New Brunswick. *New Brunswick Free Public Library Postcard Collection.*

one's home is widely viewed as a measure of achievement—as part of the American dream."

Few of John's friends had parents who owned homes. Factory workers like those employed at the Meyer Rubber Company could be expected to earn between $280 to $300 annually, depending on their skill level. A small house might cost between $200 and $500, an enormous amount of money to a factory wage earner, while the rental of four rooms cost about $5 per month. No wonder few factory workers owned homes.

Immigrants were pouring into cities to take advantage of economic opportunities, and the competition for space among residents increased housing prices, especially in fast-growing cities like New Brunswick, according to Alexander von Hoffman, senior research fellow at the Joint Center for Housing Studies, a collaborative unit between the Graduate School of Design and Harvard Kennedy School in Massachusetts. Single-family homes often were subdivided into small apartments or converted to "tenant houses" by sub-landlords, who leased the property and sublet it at a profit.

Besides the opportunity to escape from a tedious life or to respond to a patriotic call, another reason men young and old alike went to war was to earn a decent wage. A private's wage in 1861 was thirteen dollars per month, but as soldiers advanced, so did their salaries. A second lieutenant, for example, earned forty-five dollars per month; by contrast, a factory worker might make as much as fifteen to thirty dollars per month but work sixty-five to seventy hours every week. There were also financial bounties offered for reenlistment, often more money than a man could hope to earn in a year.

A home was financially out of reach for most lower- or middle-class young men. When John wrote to his mother in February 1864 about two soldier friends on furlough in New Brunswick, he explained that one was able to marry "a good steady country girl…and [bought] a good home and piece of land." This soldier, John explained, "bought it by paying a little over half cash down and the rest to be paid in installments, $20 a time." The cash came from a bounty he received when he re-enlisted that, in turn, allowed him to buy a house.

Money was also important for the family back home to maintain current living standards. John was diligent in sending his mother his army pay. It was likely that his father also sent money home since Mary Ann had to support two young girls without the income of a husband or two sons. While young James was still at home working, his wages alone could not sustain the family.

One of the exceptions to homeownership was John's best friend, Jim Furlong. An Irish immigrant who lost his mother at a young age, Jim's father owned his own home on Hamilton Street, a few blocks from the center of the city. According to the 1860 census, the Furlong home was valued at $1,500, a considerable sum. Until about 1850, city centers were the most fashionable location for merchants, lawyers and others of affluence to live. Once the Industrial Revolution arrived, the well-to-do formed exclusive enclaves and separate neighborhoods away from the center of town, leaving it to the working class.

It made sense for workers to live within walking distance of the docks, warehouses, factories, offices and shops where they worked. Those at the lowest end of the socioeconomic scale lived in the alleys and lanes of the city. Fraternal lodges, concert halls, markets, taverns and other entertainment venues were nearby.

For immigrants like the Furlongs, owning a home was an extension of their desire for social mobility. Certainly, it is a testament to the Furlong family's work ethic and effort that they were able to afford homeownership. Jim's father worked at a grocery and liquor store; Jim's brother, John Jr., twenty-three, worked as a laborer, while his nineteen-year-old sister, Mary, kept house for the family. Brother William, eighteen, along with their sister, Ann, fourteen, worked alongside Jim, seventeen, and John Hamilton at the rubber factory. Everyone contributed toward the common good, the family and the home.

The Fouretts (one of whom married into the Hamilton family) also owned a home on Neilson Street, as did a handful of others.

With the dream of property ownership in sight, Alexander Sr. joined Company D, Fifty-seventh Pennsylvania Volunteers, organized in Harrisburg, Pennsylvania, at Camp Curtain in December 1861. The New Jersey regiments were full, so anyone interested in joining the army had to travel to an adjoining state. Enlisting as a private, Alexander's army record confirmed his occupation as "farmer," not shoemaker. It is easy to speculate that Alexander, believing that he would buy property, had every intention of farming it in the future. He left with the Fifty-seventh on December 14 for Washington, D.C.

Shortly after his son's enlistment, Alexander urged John to "demand" a discharge from his colonel. Presumably, his father had a realistic sense of the dangers that were inherent in an army at war. Perhaps that was another reason his father joined: to take the responsibility of representing the family from John's shoulders. John, like a rebellious teenager, replied to his mother, "If he wants to get me out of the service, he can do it himself."

By August, more Brunswick Boys had joined John's Brigade at Camp Olden in Trenton, New Jersey. Among the ten new recruits were David Skillman, twenty-two, a machinist in the shoe factory, and John Tyler Lewis, eighteen, who worked in the rubber factory with John. John was well acquainted not only with the boys but also with their families. David Skillman Sr. was a shoemaker, and another Skillman son, John, worked with John Hamilton at the factory. John Lewis—or Tyler, as he was called—was joined in the army by his older brother, William, who also worked at the rubber factory.

The Brunswick Boys reaffirmed John's decision to enlist. With friends and acquaintances, some of home traveled with him. The other Brunswick Boy, at least by family connection, was Aleck Hamilton Jr., John's older brother. Born in 1842, Aleck enlisted in Company K, Ninth Indiana Regiment, as a second lieutenant in April. He was among the first in his state to enlist. When his enlistment period was completed after three months, he reenlisted as a private. Unfortunately, we do not know why he did not maintain his officer rank upon reenlistment.

John wrote to his mother that he was disappointed that Aleck had not tried for a commission when he reenlisted. At the start of the war, commissions were obtained in one of two ways: through political influence or by electing officers in volunteer regiments. Later, when it was found that some "officers" were either ignorant or incompetent, the Union Congress authorized creation of military boards to examine officers and remove those found to be unqualified.

In September, John saw Aleck and wrote home, "I knew him as soon as I saw him," which suggested that they had been separated for some time, John in New Brunswick and Aleck in Indiana.

Although it was not unusual for brothers, fathers and uncles from the same family to enlist, or even serve in the same regiment, the Hamilton men—Alexander Sr., Aleck, John and then James—were strung out over three states: Pennsylvania, Indiana and New Jersey. Despite that disparity, they saw one another in the next three years frequently and were able to spend time together.

More Brunswick Boys joined them. Just a year after Jim Furlong enlisted in August 1861, his brother, Bill, joined with another friend and rubber factory co-worker, George E. Fouratt. The boys joined Company F in the Eighteenth New Jersey Volunteers. It was a small world. Fouratt was brother to James Fouratt, the man who had recently married John's sister Mary Jane on January 1, 1861.

Edge Hill, Virginia
August the 7th 1861

Dear Mother,

I write you a few lines to let you know a little of the news. You see by the reading of this letter that we have changed our camp again. Night before last we got orders to be ready to march and the next morning at 10 o'clock we left camp through Alexandria to here. Some say this is Arlington Mills,[1] but most call it Edge Hill. It is 8 miles from our old camp, the one we left last.

There has been a great time in the Brigade about the time they must serve. It appears that somebody circulated a report that all regiments sworn into service before the 6th of July can only be held 3 months. If it is really the case I will be home in less than a month but I don't believe anything of the kind. Two of our lieutenants have resigned and gone home. Our lieutenant was one of them.

We are only 4 miles from the Rebs. Last night we were alarmed and turned out and formed a line of battle expecting an attack. But it was some of our pickets firing, I guess.

I received your letter and Fathers at the same time. He says in his letter that he wants me to go to my Colonel and demand a discharge. If I did not, he would make me, that is he would do it himself. I answered his letter as soon as I got it. I did not go to the Colonel and aint a-going to. If he wants to get me out of the service he can do it himself. We are having pretty good times now and not much to do but picket duty.[2]

My love to Alice & Susie and all my friends.

Your afectionate son,
John

1. Arlington Mills was near Bailey's Crossroads in present-day Arlington, Virginia.
2. Picket or sentry duty included two or more soldiers who guarded an area against enemy attack.

Camp near the Seminary, Virginia[1]
August 22nd, 1861

Dear Mother,

I received your letter last night and was surprised to hear that you had not received an answer to Alecks letter yet for I answered it as soon as I got it. The money[2] *was safe in the letter but I had to tear it nearly to pieces to get it out as it was stuck fast.*

The 4th New Jersey Regiment and Battery A, 1st N.J. got here today and are going to join our Brigade. Three days ago 10 men came from Brunswick for our regiment. Among them were David Skilman & Tiler Lewis that I know. So I see that the boys are leaving Brunswick yet to go in the army and I have made up my mind that if I were home I would not be satisfied. So I am satisfied to stay out here until the war is over.

We get one loaf of soft bread a day and fresh meat 3 times a week and I have a dangerous appetite so don't wish me home for I would eat everything in the house and then commence on the house.

I would like to see you all but the longer I am away the more of a treat it will be to see you. Tell Aleck I would like to see him. I suppose he is a six-footer now but I think I would know him.

Give my love to all.

From your son,
John

1. Camp Seminary was located near the present-day Virginia Theological Seminary outside Alexandria, Virginia.
2. Late pay: Often a soldier did not get paid on a regular basis and had to count on family at home to send funds so he could buy basic supplies from the sutler.

Camp Seminary, Virginia
Sept. the 16th 1861

Dear Mother,

I received your letter day before yesterday and was glad to hear from you. Since I wrote you last I have saw Aleck. I knew him as soon as I saw him. When he came back I came as far as Washington with him and could have deserted if I had wanted to but there is no use in deserting for you will never be able to look anyone in the face afterwards.

I have heard from Aleck. He has not got to work yet. We dont expect to have a fight here without we are attacked and then I guess we can do our share. We have got a new Colonel. His name is Torbert. He is a fine looking man about 25 years of age and a very smart officer, I think.

We have finished the fort we were building and now I dont think we will have anything to do the rest of the winter but drill and once in a while picket. We have also built a bake house and slaughter house and they talk of building barracks to winter in. I think by the papers that the war will be over by Spring and then we will all be home again.

Enclosed you will find a checque for 17 dollars to be drawn on any bank in the states. I wish you would send me a pair of pants, some dark color to change when I get wet. Send them in a little wooden box and be shure and pay for it before it leaves home. If you dont, they will charge me more than it is worth for there is a man in Co. F named Tom Curry and they charged him 2 dollars and 13 cents for a box no larger than a cigar box and home they would not dare charge anymore than 25 or 50 cents.

Jim Furlong has had the fever and ague[1] *very bad. Since I wrote you last I had a slight touch of them but it did not get a hold of me hard enough and I shook it off in 2 days.*

Give my love to all.

From your dutiful son,
John P. Hamilton

1. Ague was the name given to a type of fever marked by chills, high temperatures and sweating that recurred at regular intervals.

Chapter 3

Sutlers, Shops and the Adams Express

I received the box you sent me yesterday and was surprised and pleased to find it so well filled and nothing spoiled.

—October 28, 1861, Camp Seminary, Virginia

Throughout the war, loved ones back home sent letters and care packages to their soldier men. Mary Ann Hamilton, John's mother, packed homemade pies, wine and even a tippet (a narrow scarf for his shoulders). Other families sent only necessities like socks and boots, but many, like Mrs. Hamilton, sent anything they thought useful.

Although we only know what she sent to John from his letters, presumably she did the same for her husband, Alexander, and her other sons, Aleck and James.

At the start of the war, John was well equipped with clothing supplied by the state. He recited his personal inventory in his letter of October 18, 1861, to his mother: "3 pair of pants, 4 shirts, 5 pairs of stockings, 2 pair of drawers, 4 pocket handkerchiefs, one pair of shoes, one pair of boots, 2 caps, one woolen blanket, one rubber blanket and an overcoat."

Just a week earlier, despite his full wardrobe, John had written home requesting his mother ask a New Brunswick friend to purchase special items he did not have such as a pipe and tobacco for himself and Jim Furlong. "If he charges anything," he added, "let me know so that I can see how patriotic he is."

By late 1861, the War Department had replaced the states in outfitting and feeding soldiers, but the process was inefficient and often corrupt. In order to fill the enormous contracts to clothe hundreds of thousands of soldiers, Northern textile and shoe manufacturers cut corners and compressed "the fibers of recycled woolen goods into a material called 'shoddy,'" according to Civil War historian James M. McPherson. The word "shoddy" soon became synonymous with poorly made goods that ripped or fell apart after a few weeks. The army would have to wait until Montgomery Meigs was made quartermaster general of the army for standards to be mandated for manufacturers of clothing and other supplies.

Meigs had achieved an excellent record in the Army Corps of Engineers supervising a number of large projects, including the construction of the new Capitol dome. His work with contractors enabled him to impose "order and honesty on the chaos and corruption of early war contracts." He and the Quartermaster Bureau provided "clothing manufacturers with a series of graduated standard measurements for uniforms," introduced the concept of sizes to clothing and shoes and, whenever possible, insisted on competitive bidding.

Often, soldiers in the field or those with little money scavenged the battlefield for what they needed, removing shoes, knapsacks, weaponry and clothing from their dead compatriots or the enemy. John, who lost his shoes in a skirmish, found new ones for Furlong and himself; his father located a derringer on the battlefield, and others came away with jackets or caps to replace ones that were rotted or stolen.

When John's army-issued shoes, most probably produced under an early army contract, fell apart in the muck of a skirmish, it was a testimony to the way shoes were made, something the Hamilton men knew firsthand. Until the introduction and perfection of the Blake McKay heavy-duty shoemaking machine in 1861, sewing the soles of shoes to the uppers was either by hand sewing or lightly sewn by machine. The Blake McKay patented sewing machine revolutionized the way shoes were made, producing a sturdier shoe more quickly. With shoe demand high for both civilians and soldiers, the army used the new shoemaking method voraciously. Unfortunately, John's first pair of shoes apparently were made before the Blake McKay sewing machine went into production.

What the army did not issue to soldiers, sutlers or civilian merchants provided. These merchants sold provisions to nonmilitary personnel and soldiers in the field or in camp. Often, they set up their tents at the rear of the army or sold directly from their wagons as they traveled around camp. They monopolized the market when soldiers were in the field. Away from a town, sutlers charged high prices and garnered exorbitant profits.

The most common goods they sold were tobacco, sugar and coffee. As long as John's mother could provide additional treats, John was comfortable and could save his pay to send home. Although Mrs. Hamilton appeared to be the most generous, many of the Brunswick Boys also received items from home, like candy, socks, knitted items, reading material, cheeses, butter, preserves, whiskey, soap and other foods. Like John, they shared them among themselves. When they did have to make purchases from sutlers, the merchants did not worry about payment. Instead, any soldier owing them money had it debited from his pay. Sutlers always were present on payday.

One problem with receiving goods from home was the inconsistency of the mail. If soldiers were encamped for several weeks, letters found them easily, but for an army on the move, the continual shifting of location made delivery challenging, often being delayed by weeks. When Mary Ann Hamilton's box reached John at Camp Seminary in October 1861, the cheese she packed weeks ago had gone bad. "That cake you sent was not spoiled," John wrote, "but I cannot say as much for the cheese."

In addition, the U.S. Mail was not without issues of credibility, theft and mismanagement. On more than one occasion, John lamented that his mother did not receive the money he sent her, packages were delayed or items went missing from them. "Yesterday," he wrote in March 1863, "I got the box. It has been broken open and the jar of preserves taken out." Preserves can be replaced, but not hard-earned pay.

Northern warehouses and the railroads (or mail cars, as they were called) were also subject to theft. Allan Pinkerton, the famous nineteenth-century detective and founder of Pinkerton National Detective Agency, captured a gang of thieves in 1866 and recovered $700,000 stolen from the Adams Express Company, the same delivery service that John urged his mother to use to convey packages.

Adams Express Company, a leading independent express company incorporated in 1854, had a sterling reputation based on its involvement in delivering messages, documents and securities during the California Gold Rush and westward migration. By the time of the Civil War, it operated throughout the South with its Southern Express subsidiary. The company acted as the paymaster for soldiers on both sides, serving Union soldiers through Adams Express and the Confederates with Southern Express. If, John reasoned, Adams was secure to handle the army's payroll, then it was secure enough to handle his mother's special packages and any monies he sent home.

It was not a foolproof theory. In October 1863, while John was stationed at Centerville in Virginia, he received a box that his mother sent him by Express. "Everything in it," he wrote, "was spoiled except a little pot of butter and some cigars."

Like many of the men who came from cities, John missed the convenience of walking to the New Brunswick shops. "Give my love to the shop girls," he requested to his mother. In another letter, he wrote, "I have got socks enough to start a Jew store," a nod to some New Brunswick shops owned by Jews, particularly dry goods stores where textiles, ready-to-wear clothing and sundries were sold.

Many of the Jews who migrated to America in the mid-nineteenth century were immigrants from Germany, Poland and Hungary. Their arrival increased the size of the Jewish population in America tenfold, from 15,000 to 150,000, by 1850. Every large city felt their presence, and by 1871, Jewish families in New Brunswick had organized in a hall at Nos. 9 and 11 Peace Street and called themselves the Congregation Anshe Emett (Men of Truth).

From their European history as peddlers, it was not surprising that Jewish immigrants dominated the dry goods sector. In 1860 America, at least sixteen thousand peddlers, selling dry goods, notions, clothing and jewelry, plied their wares along the eastern seaboard. Some of these wandering peddlers settled in the small communities they serviced and opened stores. Jacob Levy's Millinery and Fine Goods store at 232 Commerce Square in New Brunswick was one such establishment that John knew and visited, as it was considered a good store to buy any piece of clothing.

There were many other shops John had frequented. In 1850, eleven years before the war, there were at least 120 shops in New Brunswick. By 1860, with a 3,000-person jump in the population to 11,256, there were probably several dozen more. There were at least five tobacconists in town, including three on Church Street, one on Peace and one on Neilson. Photography was coming into vogue at the start of the war, and there were several studios in the city. John's mother and his two sisters had their photograph taken in a photographer's studio in town and sent the image to John as a remembrance per his request.

A daily newspaper, the *New Brunswick Daily Fredonian*, and a weekly, the *Times*, were published in the city, and many of the soldiers were sent copies by family or friends or bought copies from vendors in the camps. John mentioned the *Fredonian* several times in his letters—if not by name then by the stories it published.

The city also boasted many churches, some reflecting the new immigrants. There was the Baptist church on Bayard Street; three Methodist churches; two Presbyterian; several Reformed Dutch, including St. John German

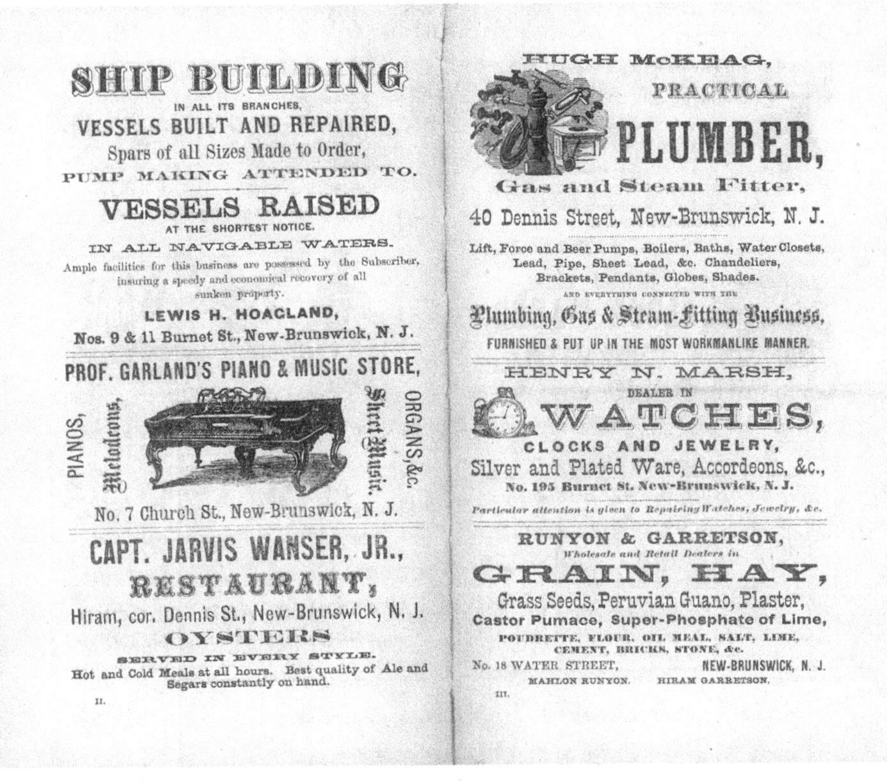

A shipbuilder, a music store and Capt. Jarvis Wanser Jr.'s Eating House, its owner a Brunswick Boy, appeared in the city directory. *New Brunswick City Directory, 1866–67.*

Reformed Dutch and German Lutheran Church; two Protestant Episcopal churches; St. Peter's and St. Paul's Roman Catholic Churches; and, of course, the newly organized synagogue.

The life of military camps was far different than living in the city. Men made do with what they had or scrambled to find something to replace it. This included making their own entertainment by playing cards, writing home, gambling, telling stories, whittling or mending their clothes. It was a lonely, isolated existence where friends replaced family and memories were fondly recalled. To some extent, the men lived vicariously through letters telling them what was occurring at home.

"Tell Jim he must write to me…and tell me about the great ball match played on Thanksgiving Day," John wrote home in December 1861. In reply, his mother reminded him of other times when the boys skated on icy New Brunswick ponds.

Letters, newspapers and soldiers returning from furlough were the lifelines to news of home. When all else failed, the Brunswick Boys had one another to talk to and comfort.

Camp Seminary, Virginia
Oct. 10th 1861

Dear Mother,

I received yours this morning while I was on picket. We have been on picket the last 3 days and this morning we were ordered to camp. We are here now. The officers are agoing to be examined. The nights are getting pretty cold here now.

While we were on picket we lived first rate. We made stews every day. We found a lot of potatoes in the barn and since then we have cooked them every style, but the best is to cut them in thin slices in some water and cut some pork up in them and let them stew until they are all in fine pieces and they make a good dinner with bread and coffee. That cake you sent was not spoiled but I cannot say as much for the cheese.

I don't know whether I can get a furlough or not, but I will try. The way the most of the men get a furlough, they get mothers or wifes to write them a letter and say that they are very sick and don't expect to live and want to see them before they die. Then they take the letter to the Colonel and show it to him but I don't like that way of getting one and if I cant get one by telling them the truth, I wont get any. I would not mind lying a little to them but not such a lie as most of them are telling.

I think we will stand a better chance for a furlough when the cold weather comes. Then we cant move anywhere and I guess they will [give] *lots of furlough then.*

I wrote a letter to Sturges to get Jim Furlong and me a pipe and match box and give them to you to send and if he charges anything for them let me know so that I can see how patriotic he is.

Your afectionate son,
John P. Hamilton

Camp Seminary, Virginia
Oct. the 28th 1861

Dear Mother,

I received the box you sent me yesterday and was surprised and pleased to find it so well filled and nothing spoiled. I am very glad you sent me those gloves and the tippet. They are just the thing I want on guard nights and on picket and we go on picket tomorrow. I am obliged to you for the pipe and other things you sent and will try to repay you with interest.

I have quite a lot of cloths now and more than I can carry if we go on a march. I will give you a list of them: 3 pair of pants, 4 shirts, 5 pair of stockings, 2 pair of draws, 4 pocket handkerchiefs, one pair of shoes, one pair of boots, 2 caps, one woolen blanket, one rubber blanket and an overcoat. Don't you think that is a load for a mule, let alone a man?

I spoke to the captain about the state pay and he says it will be all right. When Loyd Seville was home, Sailor Bill told him that he would join our company if we wanted any more men. I wrote to him and told him that we did not want more but I did not get any answer so I suppose he has backed out of it. I dont think I will try to get a furlough before New Years. I think their will be no use in trying before that time.

Those pies you sent me are the best thing I have eaten since I left home.

I have not heard from Aleck lately but I suppose he is all right. If he was not I should have heard it by this time for bad news always goes fast.

Give my love to him if you write.

From your afectionate son,
John

Chapter 4
Holidays

Here and at Home

I received your…Christmas present. One of the bottles of wine got broke and the wine soaked into the pies but did not hurt them. One the contrary, I think it improved them.

–December 29, 1861, Camp Seminary, Virginia

When the holidays arrived, loneliness and disappointment grew in the camps. Instead of anticipated merriment, the Brunswick Boys were faced with the dreary reality of camp life. There was a double reminder of missed relatives and friends as well as the lost opportunity of making new memories with families. John and the other Brunswick Boys relied on their remembrances of past holidays, as John often referred to in his letters, while they plodded through the cheerless everyday camp life and waited with anticipation for the arrival of letters and special boxes from home.

Although Thanksgiving was not yet a national holiday in November 1861, a day of thanksgiving had a long history dating to the colony at Jamestown in 1610. While the celebration varied from region to region, many American families celebrated the day with "turkey shoots" or "ball games." Brother James related a great "ball match" he played with friends on that day, while John in his letter of December 20, 1861, lamented that it would cost fourteen dollars to come home on furlough. "I don't think it would be the best way to use my money." Besides, he added, "if I got a furlough it would only be for 6 or 7 days and this is poor satisfaction for the time I was home…I would want to stay 10 days or more."

John did receive a memorable box from his mother filled with homemade pies and wine that first Christmas away from home. When one of the wine bottles broke in transit and soaked the pies, it "improved them," he told his mother.

The sending of boxes to soldiers, especially during the holidays, was memorialized by several well-known artists, including Thomas Nast and Winslow Homer. In 1861, Homer drew the first Christmas cover for *Harper's Weekly*, depicting soldiers receiving boxes from home. Packed with homemade clothing and foodstuffs, the boxes provided an emotional and physical reinforcement for the boys at camps.

Christmas also was not yet a national holiday in 1861 and was celebrated differently in various parts of the country. In some regions, it was an excuse for the working class to parade in drag or blackface, firing guns, drinking and rabble-rousing throughout the day, mimicking the pagan festival of Saturnalia, or winter's solstice. According to *New York Tribune* newspaper editor Horace Greeley, such riotous parading was typical for the city.

Other ethnic groups were beginning to celebrate with holiday parties and pageants. Small tabletop Christmas trees, a tradition made popular by Queen Victoria's German-born husband, Prince Albert, were a staple in many homes and were decorated with homemade candies and strings of popcorn and dried fruit. Although Protestants did not have special services on Christmas Day, Roman Catholics marked Christ's birth with a religious service, a Mass. Surprisingly, religious significance for the day was not yet prevalent.

For John, Christmas and New Year's presented the memories of merry times with friends and family. Although the location of Mary Ann's letters to John are unknown, John repeated her words to him in another letter. She wrote that "they have [a] fine time skating" in New Brunswick. John answered her by thanking her for the Christmas box and adding, "every day the same [here]...clean and guard," adding that there is "not much time to skate"—or celebrate, he might have added.

Another symbol of the season, the practice of gift giving, was becoming a tradition at camp and at home, too. Started by the early Dutch settlers of New York who honored St. Nicholas, stockings were hung in many homes in anticipation of St. Nicholas filling them with candy, fruit or a special treat on the eve of his feast day, December 5. The Dutch word *Sinterklaas*, for St. Nicholas, had evolved into Santa Claus by the 1820s, and Clement Clarke Moore's famous poem "The Night Before Christmas," first published in 1823, moved St. Nick's yearly gift-giving trip to Christmas Eve.

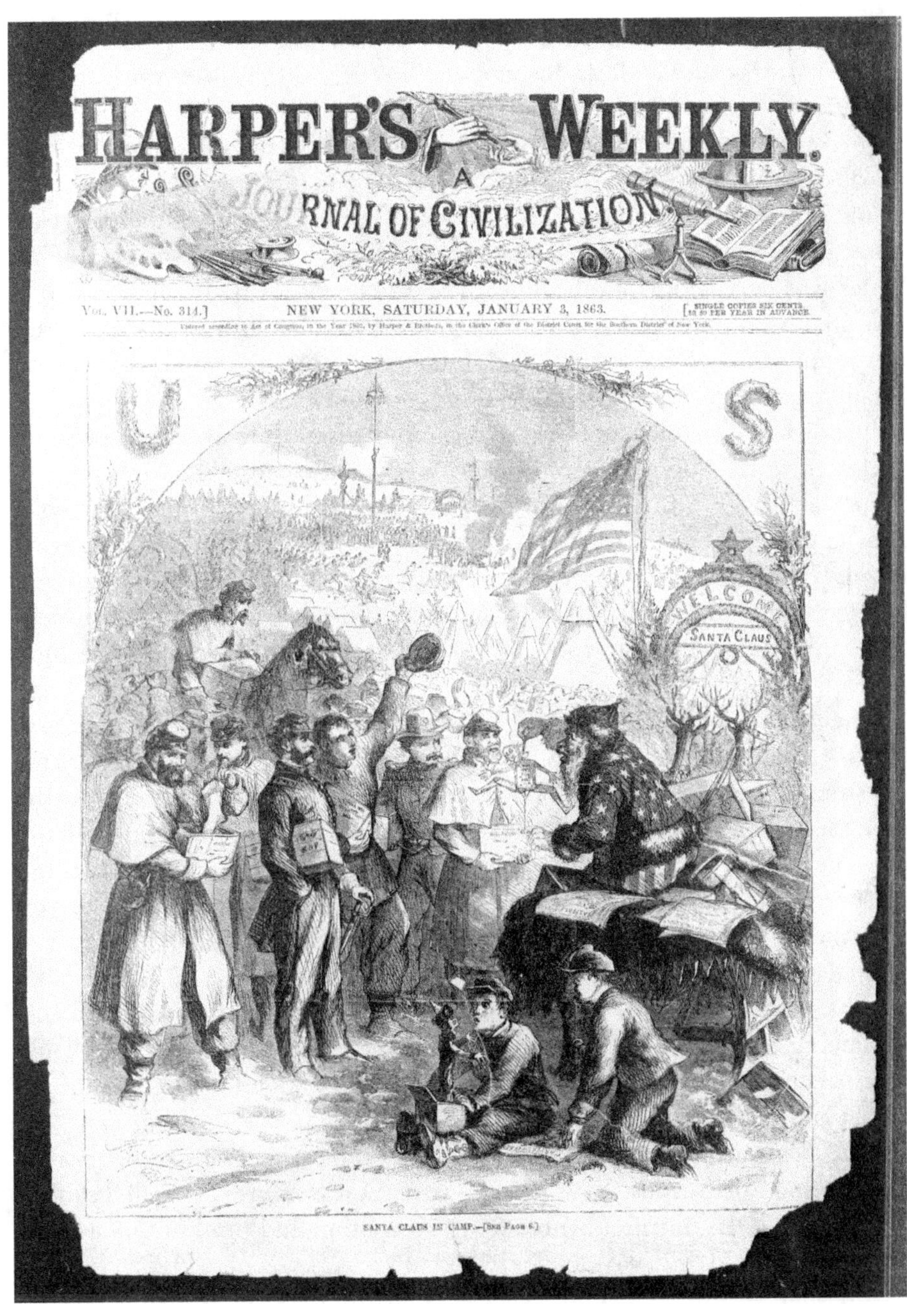

An early Thomas Nast depiction of Santa Claus showed Santa's patriotic Union costume and generosity to the Union troops. *From* Harper's Weekly, *January 3, 1863.*

By his second Christmas away from home, John had again received another Christmas box from his mother. "I received the gloves that you sent me all right and they came in good time for it is getting cold," he wrote back.

In 1863, cartoonist Thomas Nast threw his support behind Christmas by producing the first popularized illustrated drawing of a jolly, generous Santa Claus clothed in a patriotic suit of striped pants and star-spangled jacket reflecting Santa's and Nast's support for the Union. Prior to Nast's drawing, Santa was depicted as a tall, thin man. Today, Nast's merry illustration is accepted as the standard. President Abraham Lincoln and his son, Tad, were supportive of Santa, too. Tad, touched by the soldiers he visited with his father, sent gifts of books and clothing to many soldiers.

"It will be Christmas soon," John reminded his mother in mid-December. To lessen worries about him, he wrote to sister Mary Jane that they were in a fine camp at White Oak Church in Stafford County, Virginia. "We have a large piece of canvas for the roof and it is very comfortable. We have a fireplace in it but we do not require any fire yet for it is quite warm yet, but the nights are cool." Lest she think he did not miss home, he added, "The time passes very slow in camp. I wish you would send me something to read."

The following year, 1863, was John's last Christmas away from home, and his longing and loneliness become apparent in his letter to his fourteen-year-old sister, Susan. "I suppose," he wrote a few days before Christmas, "by the time this reaches you, it will be Christmas and I hope you will all enjoy it and New Year's also. If I were home, I would give you all some nice presents but out here I cannot buy anything for you so I will send a little money for you and Alice to buy something for yourselves...You can buy more with this than I could out here with $5.00." It was a generous gift.

"You and Alice," he directed Susan, "can go downtown and buy something...and it will be the same as if I were there and gave it to you." The longing and nostalgia of the season was revealed by his comment, "That is if you can only think so."

John then recalled past holidays and was swept away by those memories. "I can remember the last New Year's Day that I was home very well. I started from home in the morning with a new overcoat on and Jim Furlong and his brother were with me...We had a jolly day."

Although a little late, John received Christmas boxes from his mother and his sister Mary Jane in early January. "[I]...was very much pleased with them and you bet I had a fine lot of good things. Everything was in order in both boxes."

Later that month, he sent his sister Susan a small locket with his picture in it, a tender gesture. "I found it [the locket] some time ago," he explained to his mother, "and was agoing to send it to her for a New Year's present but I did not have the money to have the picture taken."

In an action foreshadowing O. Henry's famous 1906 short story, *The Gift of the Magi*, John demonstrated his generosity in buying a gift. "I sold my watch for 10 dollars" to buy it, he said, adding, as justification, "it would not run so it was no use to me." If, indeed, the watch was broken, who would pay ten dollars dollars for it? It is more likely that John made up the story about the broken watch so his mother would not feel guilty about his generosity. John's kind act will be reciprocated later when a photograph is sent to him.

Anticipating his younger sister's response to the gift, he asked his mother to "tell Alice she must not be jealous of Susan because I sent her the locket. I sent it to her [Susan] because she is the oldest."

Camp Seminary, Virginia
Dec.11th 1861

Dear Mother,

I received your letter and also the box. The boots just fit me so I can put 2 pair of stockings on with them. I have got stockings enough to start a Jew store. I don't think there is anything else I want now.

You say you are a going to send me a Christmas dinner. Dont send anything that will spoil.

When you write tell me how much you paid for the boots and tell me what Regiment Father enlisted in for there is some Pennsylvania Regiments around here and he may be in among them.

Tell Jim he must write to me and tell me about that great ball match played on Thanksgiving Day and tell him if he knows as much as I do about soldiering he wont bother his head about coming out. If he is once sworn into the service, he must do a soldiers duty whether he likes it or not.

Love to all.

Your son,
John

Camp Seminary, Virginia
Dec. 29th 186l

Dear Mother:

I received your letter and Christmas present the day after Christmas. One of the bottles of wine got broke and the wine soaked into the pies but did not hurt them. On the contrary I think it improved them. I divided with Furlong but he dont care as much as the eatables as he does the wine.

I spent my Christmas on guard but every day is the same out here. Last 4th of July I was marching part of the day, the rest of the day I was in Congress listening to the Senators and the next I hope to spend home. I answered your last letter while I was on picket and suppose you have got it by this time. I told you about that man getting shot for deserting and I suppose you saw the picture of it in the Illustrated Newspaper. If you did it looks just as it did when I saw him shot.

Our lieutenant left here for home on 7 days furlough and I suppose he has passed through Brunswick before this gets to you.

We have not much to do now but clean and guard the camp and drill and do picket—but that keeps us as busy as we want to be. As I have some more room I will write Jim a little.

From your afectionate son,
John

Dear Brother James,

Having some room to spare I thought I would write you a few lines. I am sorry to hear that you have left the store for I think it was the best place you could be for you could learn to write and keep books very fast.

Mother says that you have got it into your head that you want to get with Aleck in the army. Dont you do it, Jim for I think that is enough if we are all in the army, but you and yours had better stay home and go back to your place again or do anything but soldier for you are too young to soldier for it is no easy life, I can assure you.

I am glad you beat the club playing ball and hope you will beat everything that you play with. Dont leave home, Jim.

From your afectionate brother,
John P. Hamilton

Camp Seminary, Virginia
Jan 14th 1862

Dear Mother:

I received your letter and was glad to hear from you. I received my pay on the 10th. I am going to see if I can get a furlough and if I cant, I will send my money home. I don't have much hope of getting one, but I will try.

So you think when we are on picket we are in a dangerous place. Sometimes we are when we are on the outposts. But then we keep our eyes open and dont let the Rebs get the advantage of us. We have been troubled some with Bushwhackers shooting our pickets in the night. I suppose you dont know what a Bushwhacker is. They are farmers that live around her and in the day time they are as innocent as lambs and good union men and as soon as it gets dark, they take their rifle and sneak on our pickets and shoot them by the light of their picket fire.

These are worse than Reb soldiers for they hardly ever shoot at each other in the night for I have been on post where I could see the rebel picket walking past his fire and, of course, he could see me, but we did not fire at each other.

You say they have fine times skating in Brunswick. I cant say as much for there aint been ice thick enough to hold a dog and if there was, we would not have much time to skate.

I am sorry to hear that James has still got soldiering in his head and hope he will change his mind and stay home.

Tell Susie I think she is improving in her writing and Alice must be a smart girl to write her name so well. Give my love to them and James.

From your afectionate son,
John.

Chapter 5
THE TINDERBOX CITY

I heard of the large fire you had in Brunswick. It must have been a grand sight.
–February 6, 1862, Camp Seminary, Virginia

The city of New Brunswick, like all American cities at the start of the Industrial Revolution, endured the growing pains of an expanding population. From 1810 to 1860, more than 5.0 million immigrants came to America—4.2 million of them arriving between 1840 and 1860. Three-fourths of these new Americans were either German or Irish, and New Brunswick reflected this influx. Some of the better educated found jobs readily, while others found employment as servants or as factory workers. Many of the men and boys, such as Alexander Hamilton and his sons, John and James, worked in the rubber factory with Irish immigrants, including John's best friend, Jim Furlong.

New Brunswick offered jobs where few language or mechanical abilities were needed. Basic skills, sometimes just brawn, were acceptable in the rubber factories, ironworks, cotton mills and wallpaper manufacturers of the city. More experienced and seasoned craftsmen within these industries received higher pay.

The workingman and his family lived close to the place they worked, often in overcrowded tenements or row houses. These flimsy structures, hastily built of wood, often lacked adequate air circulation, light or sanitary conditions. They were rented to them by landlords who were uncaring of how many people lived in one room. While this level of poverty was stigmatizing, there was an even greater enemy for the poor: fire.

Baltimore's Big Fire of 1904 was typical of city fires. It spread quickly and took more than thirty hours to extinguish. *Library of Congress.*

The Liberty Hose Company was one of several fire companies in the city. *New Brunswick Free Public Library Postcard Collection.*

Urban fires and wildfires were common in mid-nineteenth-century American cities. In 1835, New York City was ravaged by fire; ten years later, fire consumed Pittsburgh, Pennsylvania. Nantucket, Massachusetts, was destroyed in 1846, and St. Louis, Missouri, and San Francisco, California, followed a few years later. Some cities, like Portsmouth, New Hampshire, endured multiple great fires in 1802, 1805, 1813 and again in 1835.

New Brunswick was no stranger to citywide fires. In 1768, a fire, fanned by high winds, destroyed five homes, a bakeshop, a bottling factory and a copper shop. Then, in 1796, a much larger fire engulfed the entire city. It was reported that the damage was so extensive that the state appropriated $5,000 for the victims, an amount of aid unheard of for that time.

By 1860, the city had thirty-nine wells for use in quenching fires along with a growing fire department. Washington Engine Company No. 1 was organized in 1705, and although it had no firefighting apparatus in its early years, it supplied each of its members with a large bucket. The New Brunswick Hook and Ladder Company, organized in 1835, also began as a bucket brigade, later procuring a wheeled hose cart. In 1863, the Liberty Hose Company was formed using an old horse carriage formerly belonging to the Phoenix Hose Protection Engine Company No. 6, which was first organized in 1817 and then reorganized in 1852.

They used hand pumps until the first steamer-driven pump, a Haupt, was available in 1867. The engine designer, Jacob L. Haupt of Philadelphia, built these steam machines with two single-acting pumps. They weighed more than six thousand pounds, a formidable weight for men or horses to carry to a fire.

Well-meaning but ineffective firefighting companies could not completely protect the tinderbox-like city. Fires were disastrous because of the flammable building materials of the day and overcrowding. They were overwhelming in their path of destruction.

On January 15, 1862, such a fire caught in one of the most densely built-up and populated areas of the city, Commerce Square. As John wrote in his letter home of February 6, "I heard of the large fire you had…it must have been a grand sight." He may have read about it in the *New Brunswick Daily Fredonian*, which reported the event the next day in its January 16 edition. Perhaps one of the Brunswick Boys received the paper from a family member or a returning soldier from leave brought the news into camp.

The fire was discovered at about 1:00 a.m. by a night watchman, who noticed a "bright light" in Jacob Levy's Millinery and Fine Goods store at 232 Commerce Square. When the watchman investigated, according to the newspaper report, "he found the store on fire and immediately rattled the door to awake those in the building…shouting 'Fire.'"

The Levy family, who resided above the store, and their next-door neighbors, the Armstrongs, escaped just in time, unscathed, but without any property or clothes. The fire spread quickly throughout the block, destroying eight stores, including the Levy's, William H. Armstrong's Store of Tin Ware, John Diamond's Fancy Goods and Johnson and Schrenck's Boots. Multiple families were left homeless.

In all, more than $60,000 of property, equivalent today to $220,000, was estimated to have been destroyed in flames—this time, fortunately, without loss to life. The *Fredonian* urged the women of the city to respond to the needs of the ladies who were victims to the fire by supplying clothing.

John's reaction was somewhat more visionary. "I suppose," he wrote his mother, "it is a good thing to burn some of those old houses there now." Indeed, city fires transformed housing through a painful urban renewal process. The destruction of rickety wooden homes necessitated relocation of the lower social classes to different urban neighborhoods. Rebuilding in fire-ravaged areas attracted both new industries and the affluent.

Camp Seminary, Virginia
Feb 6th 1862

Dear Mother,

I received your always welcome letter yesterday and was glad to hear from you and all the family. I am glad you sent me such a long letter. The boys laughed at it and said I had a Brunswick newspaper. I read it over twice and wished it was twice as long. I would write you a long one in return but I cant find news interesting enough to make a long letter.

I am surprised to see how good Susan can write. She can beat me all to pieces and Alice aint very far behind her. I wish you would take some weekly paper and after you read it send it to me every week. It will help pass the long evenings away.

I heard of the large fire you had in Brunswick. It must have been a grand sight and I suppose it is a good thing to burn some of those old houses there now.

When I received your letter last night I received one from Aleck at the same time. He is still recruiting at Logan and says it is slow business. They dont average one recruit a week. That is pretty slow recruiting but I dont think we want many more soldiers for I think we have got enough now to put the rebellion down in the spring for this is a fine army and well drilled and when they all get a moving, it will have to be something pretty big to stop them.

It is reported around here that the Pennsylvania and New Jersey troops are a going to be kept here on the Potomac in reserve. But I dont believe it and if the army moves I hope we will go with them and I will bet that our one armed General Kearney[1] *wont be left behind if he can help it.*

I received a letter from Mary Jane the other day. She wrote no news in particular only baby and the rest were well. I suppose that before this reaches you, you will receive my photograph. I sent it about 3 days ago. I am sorry I did not put my side arms on as the jacket looks too big for me but it looks like the original and that is all that is required. You wanted to know how those pants were holding out that you sent me. They are holding out good for I aint wore them 4 hours since I had them. They are in my knapsack as good as when I received them.

I am glad that James has gone back to the store again and hope he will not get soldiering on the brain anymore. Give my love to brother and sisters.

From your afectionate son,
John P. Hamilton

1. General Philip Kearny had lost an arm during the Mexican-American War.

Camp Seminary, Virginia.
Feb 15th, 1862

Dear Mother:

I received your welcome letter yesterday. I like the story in the weekly. First rate! It is rumored that we are going to advance on Monday. The roads are pretty good now. We would have advanced before this if they had not been so bad. They say that General McClellan[1] *is a going to have charge of the advance in person. If we get marching orders before you answer this I will let you know. Their was a great time here when we got the news of the capture of Roanoke Island.*[2] *The whole army were cheering at once and it made a racket, you had better believe.*

We have brigade drill every day except Wednesday and Saturday with our knapsacks on, but they aint very heavy if they are packed right, although I have a pretty solid knapsack when my things are all packed into it. I have got all the cloths I want.

I have not heard from Aleck since I wrote you last nor have I heard from Father. There is some Pennsylvania Regiments in our division but the 57th is not among them. I should not be surprised if his regiment had gone on some of those expeditions.

I received the postage stamps and am obliged to you for them although I had plenty at the time for I always buy enough every pay day to last me until I am paid again.

I am getting to be a regular Dutchman. I can understand a good deal of their talk and eat their stinking chese and I think if I eat enough of it I can talk Dutch as fast as any of them.

Give my love to Jim, Susie, Alice and Mother.

Your absent
John P. Hamilton

1. General George B. McClellan commanded the Union Army of the Potomac, and until March 11, 1862, he was general-in-chief of all Federal armies.
2. On February 8, Federal forces attacked and defeated Confederate troops on Roanoke Island, North Carolina.

Camp Seminary, Virginia
March the 5th, 1862

Dear Mother,

I write you a few lines to let you know a little of the news. The day before I came in from picket I heard that Father had been in camp looking after me and he had left his directions in Company F where I could find him. So yesterday morning I got a pass to go and find him and after traveling 8 miles I found him. He was very glad to see me. He looks very well. He is the oldest man in the company. They call him Elder.

It appears that he has had quite a time in trying to find me. He always looked for me in cavalry and that is the reason he had so much trouble to find me. He said he had made his mind up not to write to you until he had found me. He was 4 days away from camp at one time looking for me and always in cavalry. He, at last, found out by accident. He happened to get in the 1st New Jersey Calvary and there were several knew me and where I was. So the next day he came to our camp and as his luck I was on picket and so he had to go back without seeing me.

He has been talking to me about that place he has picked out in Pennsylvania and showed me letters describing the place and I think we had better buy it and then we will have a home of our own.

Father dont like his officers. His Colonel left the Regiment the other day to get clear of being court mashalled. The regiment lay near Fort Lyon. He is in the 57th Pennsylvania Volts Co. D, Captain Calkins' Company.

He told me to give his love to you and the children. We expect to move soon.

Love to all from your absent son,
John

Chapter 6
Bosom Friends

I stopped and got a pair [of shoes] *for myself and a pair for Furlong as I knew he wanted a pair.*
—July 18, 1862, camp near Harrison Landing, Virginia

Side by side, Jim Furlong and John worked together at the rubber factory in New Brunswick, socialized with each other and shared a common background. Both had Irish mothers, and although Jim was motherless, it is easy to imagine Mary Ann Hamilton welcoming Jim into her home as one of her son's best friends. Not only were the boys inseparable at home, but they also joined the volunteers together, traveling to Trenton in 1861. Of all the Brunswick Boys, Jim Furlong was, by far, John's best and closest friend.

The boys lived in the same New Brunswick ward, and it is likely that Mrs. Hamilton even shopped at Jim's father's grocery store. His industrious father, John Furlong, emigrated from Ireland in 1850 with his oldest son, John Jr. After the elder Furlong established his business—and while oldest son, John Jr., worked as a laborer—Mr. Furlong sent to Ireland for the rest of his children. Once here, oldest daughter Mary kept house, while William and Jim worked in the rubber factory with their fourteen-year-old sister, Ann.

When Jim arrived on the ship *Great Western* from Liverpool in May 1854, his father had already set the groundwork for a prosperous business. There was little time to socialize for the hardworking family, but at every opportunity, Jim and John were together. Jim's brother William, just a year younger, often tagged along. He even joined the war a short year after his brother.

It is apparent that the boys pledged to stick together and help each other after they enlisted in the army. Incident after incident that John wrote about in his letters, from sharing food to seeking replacement shoes, made it clear that they were watching out for each other. John even reported Jim's health to his mother as if she were his friend's mother, too. "Jim has had the fever and ague very bad," he wrote in one letter, adding, almost as an afterthought, "I had a slight touch of them but it did not get hold of me hard enough and I shook it off in two days."

When Furlong became ill again in August 1862, John wrote to his mother, reassuring her. "Furlong has not been very well lately but is better now." Furlong was like another son to Mrs. Hamilton, and certainly the motherless Furlong felt her tenderness and was comforted by it and John's care of him.

John included Jim's requests for items from home with his own, asking his mother to have a friend, Sturges, send Jim and him a pipe and matchbox. Indeed, when John's Christmas box of wine and pies arrived, he made a point to tell his mother, "I divided with Furlong…he don't care as much as the eatables as he does the wine." There was no question that Jim was part of the Hamilton family.

Food was an important, sometimes scarce commodity in war, and to share it with another was an act of generosity. In March 1862, while the boys were at Camp Seminary, John related how he and Jim and some others went from camp to a farmhouse to have breakfast. "We got ham and eggs, hot biscuits and butter and coffee so that was a treat to us." To break bread with your friends from home was especially comforting. He added that the people who made them breakfast were "glad we drove the Rebs back." It was probably a gesture of thankfulness and hospitality to feed the boys even though the price of food was high.

Shoes were also an uncommon, costly commodity. When John fought in a skirmish near Harrison Landing close to Richmond in July 1862, he dashed through a mud hole, and his untied shoes became stuck and lost. He wrote home, "I had not got outside of the woods," he wrote, "before I came to some knapsacks and some shoes were hanging to them. And I stopped and got a pair for myself and a pair for Furlong as I knew he wanted a pair."

The knapsacks may have been left by Rebels, who found them too heavy to carry while retreating. When the Rebels reappeared shooting their muskets, they killed "nearly all the horses. The wounded horses turned and came back like mad with their heads up in the air." John had one purloined shoe on and the other three under his arm. "I saw them coming towards me so I jumped into a lot of ivy bushes to get clear of them but they came right over me and knocked me down and trampled me in the mud…they did not hurt me much," he added, but the shoes and cap did not fare as well. The horses "threw the shoes and my cap so far in the mud that I could not find them and…it was getting dark. I had no trouble to get a cap in the company, but I could not get any shoes."

Later, John had better luck obtaining food for his friends. When the regiment was ordered to fall back to Harrison's Landing after the Seven Days' Battles in June/July 1862, John discovered "a large pile of cracker boxes" at the edge of the river. "Crackers," or hardtack, was the staple food of the war. Made of flour, water and often salt, they were thick and hard as a brick. They were not popular among soldiers, who called the food "digestable leather," "angel cakes," "teeth dullers" or "ammo reserves."

"The guard," he wrote to his mother, "told us to help ourselves and I filled my shirt around my waist and all my pockets and hat besides putting a good share inside of my ribs. It was raining as hard as it could pour down. By the time I got back to camp I was as wet as a drowned rat and the crackers were all soft but the men were all crazy to get one…I gave them all away but enough for me and Furlong to eat."

We can only imagine how Furlong reciprocated John's kindnesses with acts of friendship. In late August, as the boys traveled to Newport News, Virginia, during the Federal retreat from Richmond, they found an ingenious way to eat the famous crabs of the region. Perhaps it was Jim's idea that they put their bayonets on their guns and walk along the shore "until we saw one [crab] close to shore and then we would stick the bayonet through him. In this way we caught all we wanted in a short time." It must have been a memorable meal.

By September 1862, John and Jim's regiment was on the move via Manassas through Crompton's Pass to the large-scale battle at Antietam, Maryland. "Our position," he related, was "under a galling fire of both artillery and infantry…the Rebels shelled us all day."

It is during the bloodiest single day of the war at Antietam/Sharpsburg that Furlong was struck by a shell in his shoulder. It was a serious wound. Furlong's injury was reported on the official casualty sheet, according to his war records at the National Archives. John predicted that it would require a month or two for him to recover. It was probably during this same battle that Furlong performed an act of bravery and courage that prompted his brevet promotion to full corporal the next month.

Due to the seriousness of his wound, Furlong likely was transported to a hospital. He may have stayed a month or two, or he could have been sent home to recuperate, which was a common occurrence. The record is incomplete as to what he actually did and where he recuperated.

Photographer Alexander Gardner depicted the carnage of Antietam, where more than twenty-two thousand Union and Confederate soldiers were killed, wounded or reported missing. *Library of Congress.*

While the promotion to full corporal was noted in Furlong's service record, it was an honorary promotion given in recognition of gallant conduct or meritorious service and was practically meaningless in terms of real authority or increased pay.

Company K, the boys' company, was disbanded in October 1862 due to the loss of men and leadership that occurred at Antietam in September. "Our General was wounded and has since died," John wrote to his mother. "I think we lost two thirds of the Brigade. Most of them were taken prisoners. Our company are all missing, but 13. We know that 3…are killed and 43… are wounded so the brigade was pretty well used up and discouraged."

The two inseparable boys decided to stay together. Both John and Jim were transferred officially to Battery A, First Regiment New Jersey, Light Artillery. Furlong transferred in as a corporal, but John was once again a private.

From their transfer into the artillery until their discharge, there is no more mention of Furlong in John's letters. They may have been assigned different duties in the regiment and so were not in daily contact with each other, or they may have had a temporary minor disagreement. However, they continued to serve together in the same artillery division, fighting and sharing in the sorrows to come.

Furlong did not receive a medical discharge, but he was mustered out at the end of his term of service in June 1864 at the same time as his bosom friend. He and John returned to New Brunswick together, bound by a friendship forged even stronger by the war.

Steamboat Hero on the Potomac
April 9th, 1862

Dear Mother,

We are now on the water and bound for somewhere.[1] *I dont know where but anything for a change. When I wrote you last, you remember I was at Cedar Creek. The next day after I wrote you we got orders to march back to Alexandria and in 2 days we marched it and day before yesterday we embarqued on board this steamer. Some say we are going as far as Fort Munroe. On our march back to Alexandria we passed the battle field of Bull Run and saw several skeletons of men that had not been buryed. Several of the graves had been opened. I suppose by the friends to get the bodys.*

I wish you would send me some money as I am out and dont know when we will be paid. I would not want any only we are going in a strange country and I dont know how much good it will do me.

We have slept 2 nights on the Potomac and I suppose we will sleep tonight as there is no signs of our stopping yet.

I dont suppose I will have a chance to send this letter until we do get on shore. I think I would like the navy better than the land services. We passed Mount Vernon and I saw the tomb of Washington. The band played Old Hundred[2] *while we passed. I also saw the battery that the Rebs made on the banks of the Potomac to blockade Washington.*

I will write you as soon as we stop somewhere. Direct your letters as before and they will follow us.

Give my love to all.

From your absent son,
John P. Hamilton

1. General McClellan had embarked the Army of the Potomac onto boats to be transported to Hampton, Virginia, in an attempt to attack Richmond by outflanking the Confederate forces.
2. "Old Hundred" is an old psalm (circa 1551) and one of the best-known melodies in Christian music.

Camp near Shipping Point, Virginia[1]
April 29th, '62

Dear Mother,

You see by the heading of this that I am on land again. I received your letter with a 5 dollar bill yesterday and it came very handy as I was out of tobacco. But I did not want so much. 2 dollars would have been plenty. There is a sutler here and he charges 40 cents for a small plug of tobacco.

I have not heard from Father yet but I suppose we will all be together in this next Battle at Yorktown and if I hear from him I will let you know. We hear heavy firing in the direction of Yorktown night and day.

I will write as soon as I get another opportunity.

Love to all from you son,
John Hamilton

1. John may have stopped at Shipping Point earlier; however, he did not hear heavy firing from Yorktown while at that location. Shipping Point is south of Washington, D.C., where the Quantico River meets the Potomac; it is nearly 150 miles north of Yorktown by boat. He was probably nearer to Fort Monroe, close to Hampton, Virginia.

Chapter 7
A WHOLE SKIN

I take this opportunity of informing you that I have a whole skin yet and have not been any very dangerous place since I wrote you last.
—June 6, 1862, Gaines's Mill, Virginia

I could count six dead rebels almost in reach of me and as the day before had been so hot, they smell awful, but we had to stand it as it was almost death to move and besides it would be hard to find a place on that field that was not pretty well covered with dead. It was the worse sight I have saw yet.
—September 20, 1862, camp on the South Mountain, Maryland

The Brunswick Boys' family and friends kept abreast of the war news via the newspaper and official war notifications of the dead and wounded. "Keeping a whole skin" became a mantra for John, as was "dodging bullets." Sometimes he avoided them, but at other times, their paths converged dangerously close. His father and youngest brother were less fortunate. The ammunition used often determined the seriousness of the casualty.

Buckshot created devastating wounds if not outright death. In May 1862, John wrote to his mother that six men, although none was a Brunswick Boy, were wounded in his regiment, most mortally "as most of them were buckshot wounds." Shotguns often were used by the Confederates. They had enormous energy, especially at close range, and their coarse lead shot inflicted serious damage.

Just one month later in June, four miles outside Richmond during the Peninsula Campaign (the first Union attempt to capture the Confederate capital), the Rebels attacked as John's regiment prepared for a dress parade. "If brother James could have been there," he wrote to impress his younger brother, "and saw the limbs getting cut off of the trees over his head and the pieces of shell flying around his head, he would have come to the conclusion to not go a soldiering."

Rifled cannons, with their spiral grooves inside the cannon barrel, allowed the shell to spin and added incredible force to knock limbs off trees and heads off shoulders.

At the Battle of Chickahominy/Gaines's Mill on June 27, 1862, John had a close encounter with enemy fire. Having lost the location of his own brigade, commanded by Brigadier General George Taylor, John advanced with the Fifth New York Zouaves Regiment, an elite unit called Duryee's Zouaves after its first colonel, Abram Duryee. The Zouaves, known for their distinctive short open-fronted jacket and baggie trousers, were praised at Gaines's Mill for their efficiency and drill in the thickest fight. Facing the worse firing force from enemy Confederate troops, the Zouave Regiment lost one-third of its men.

"The nearest I came to getting hit that I know was once I went to take aim from behind a tree and a ball hit the trees within an inch of my face; the bark hit me in the eyes and I thought at the time that I was wounded but I came out all right." John narrowly missed being shot from a rifle, probably the most commonly used gun in the war and also known for its accuracy and range. Luckily for John, the Rebel who fired it must not have been an expert shot.

According to the after-action report lodged by General George W. Taylor later that month, the First Regiment entered the woods, where a "fierce combat was raging…they were all the time under a galling fire often a crossfire," so it was not difficult to understand how John became separated from his company.

A few days later, John reconnected again with his father, Alexander. Father and son had been searching for each other ever since Alexander's Fifty-seventh Pennsylvania Regiment had moved into Virginia in early 1862. Alexander joined the Pennsylvania regiment sometime in late 1861, and although father and son exchanged at least one letter, they never met. "I have not found Father, yet," John reported to his mother on March 2, 1862. Likewise, Alexander had trouble finding his son. "He has so much trouble to find me he said he had made his mind up not to write to you until he had found me."

On March 5, 1862, John learned that the Fifty-seventh Regiment was nearby. He obtained a pass and traveled eight miles, finding his father in camp. "He was very glad to see me. He looks very well," he wrote home, adding, "He is the oldest man in the company. They call him Orderly Elder." It came as no surprise to his mother. She remembered too well that her husband was forty-nine-years-old.

Father and son had a heartfelt meeting. Alexander shared that he had found land in Pennsylvania and showed his son letters describing the area. John, in turn, was excited by the prospect. "I think we had better buy it and then we will have a home of our own." Alexander also shared his distaste for his officers. "His Colonel left the Regiment the other day to get clear of being court marshaled," John wrote.

Separated by war, the two met again when their regiments converged near Richmond after the Battle of Fair Oaks on May 31, 1862. Alexander had been wounded in the left thigh and sustained injuries to his spine and kidneys from being run over by his own troops, according to his pension records at the National Archives. Walking with a crude stick, Alexander came into his son's camp. "He could not get in an ambulance as they were all full," John explained.

Alexander may have been hit by the dreaded Minié ball, the most damaging rifle bullet used in the war. Most soldiers who were hit by one in a limb lost the limb if not their life. Made of lead, the Minié ball traveled at a high velocity and was accurate at two hundred to three hundred yards. As the projectile traveled to its target, it spun from the rifled barrel and would "deform and tumble on impact," according to Janet King, writing in *Civil War Medicine.* "Its effect on bone and tissue," Ms. King wrote, "was incredibly devastating. It would smash, tear apart, and disintegrate what it hit. Most of the amputations that occurred were because of this great devastation."

Alexander was able to make John breakfast when his son returned from nighttime picket duty, but he was unable to keep up with him on the march from camp. In one of the most touching scenes of his letters, John was forced to leave his father. "They would not let me stay behind with him [Alexander]," he wrote. "So we soon got ahead of him and I have not seen him since." Sadly, John and his father would be separated even longer, for Alexander was sent first to Alexandria, Virginia, and then home to New Brunswick to recover from his injuries.

John again reunited with his company, which thought him dead, as it moved farther south during a retreat ordered by General George McClellan through Frayser's Farm toward Harrison's Landing, Virginia. It is here where

Illustrator Winslow Homer depicted a surgeon at work during the battle at Fair Oaks. *From* Harper's Weekly, *July 1862.*

A Matthew Brady photograph of the convalescent camp near Alexandria, Virginia, where Alexander Hamilton was sent before returning home. *Library of Congress.*

the Confederate army caught the company on June 30 and where John's regiment joined a "hard fight" led by General Kearny. "We run about 2 miles through the woods. The artillery of the enemy engaged with Kearny's Division and their shell came bouncing through the woods past us. Some of the men were killed by them."

Months later, on September 14, 1862, at the Battle at Crampton's Gap/Burkittsville in Maryland, the Union army was pursuing the Rebel army's invasion of the North in Maryland. It was here where John again narrowly avoided death. As the regiment advanced through a mountain defile called Crampton's Gap, where the Confederates were positioned, John wrote that he was surprised they did not put up a fight. The Confederates "threw their arms down and went to the rear and as soon as we formed our line we started up the hill…we had not got far before the second line of Rebs opened a volley on us and I got hit on the head and knocked down but was up again in a minute and feeling of my head no blood, I went ahead."

As the men gave chase after the Rebel squad, John met the enemy face to face. "When just as we were passing a tree that had blown down with the roots sticking up in the air, a rebel stepped from behind the roots and fired his rifle in my face, so close was he that I could not see for some minutes." John's first reaction, after he realized that he was alive, was anger at the Rebel, not for shooting him, but because in taking the shot he had no chance to escape. "[S]ome of our fellows had taken him prisoner. If he had been in front of me when I got my eyes open I do believe I would have shot him for he had no right to shoot when he saw he had no chance to get away. He must have been so excited," John reasoned that "he did not know what he was doing."

That night, John examined his head and found "a lump about as large as my fist and part of my hat gone. I think the ball struck a stone in front of me and flattened and stuck me flat on the head or else it was the stone. I don't know which." Once again, John had a "whole skin." John's best friend, Jim Furlong, was not as lucky.

As the regiment moved on to the Battle of Antietam/Sharpsburg on September 17, 1862, to attack the Confederate army invading Maryland, the men were subject to "a galling fire of both artillery and infantry…When we got our position, we lay down and then it was not so bad as the enemy could not see us. Jim Furlong got hit on the shoulder by a piece of shell…I suppose he will get over it in 4 or 5 weeks." Furlong was sent to an army hospital for a long recuperation. He had an almost "whole skin."

The Confederates did not fare well either in the single bloodiest day of the war. That night, while John was on the skirmish line fifty yards from the

John was assigned to a twenty-pound Parrott gun in the artillery, although larger sizes, such as the one-hundred-pound Parrott, also were used in the war. *Library of Congress.*

Rebels, he related to his mother, "I could count six dead rebels almost in reach of me and as the day before had been so hot, they smelt awful, but we had to stand it as it was almost death to move and besides it would be hard to find a place on that field that was not pretty well covered with dead. It is the worse sight I have saw yet."

John's company, too, was affected by the loss of men on the battlefield. By October 1862, the company had disbanded because its officers were dead and only thirteen privates, including John, remained fit for duty. He was transferred in October 1862 to light artillery, and although the battery captain asked John to take charge of two horses, he chose instead to be a cannoneer, "for it is so much trouble to take care of horses in cold weather." He liked his new assignment. "We can march easy," he told his mother, "as the men do not carry knapsacks or muskets."

One of his first artillery engagements was at the Battle of Fredericksburg in December 1862. To alleviate his mother's fears of his new assignment, he wrote that he was well and then, like a thoughtless teenager, related a dangerous artillery battle. "Yesterday our section was sent down…to silence

4 of the rebels' guns that was annoying the Infantry. We were in full view of them and had only 2 guns and they made the gravel fly around."

Assigned to William Hexamer's New Jersey Battery at Fredericksburg, the light artillery was situated close to the Rappahannock River. "They had the advantage of us because the wind blew toward us and every time they fired, the smoke was between them and us and by the time the smoke cleared away they would be loaded again...We would have to stand up in open sight and load." Within an hour, they ran. "We lost 3 horses," he reported, "but none of our men got hit."

Months later, when Fredericksburg was taken in May 1863 during the campaign of Chancellorsville, John recalled how the Rebels charged their battery three times. The Union used canister shot or case shot in its cannons, a closed cylindrical metal canister typically filled with round lead or iron balls. When fired, the canister disintegrated and its projectiles spread out, causing a wide path of destruction. At very close range, artillery crews fired lethal "double canister," where two rounds were loaded into the gun tube and fired using a single charge:

> *The last time they charged they came very close to us but every man stood by the guns and we were giving them double rounds of canister...we worked in our shirt sleeves at the guns steady from about 3 o'clock until after dark and our guns were so hot that the black paint on them was all blisters... We all had some very narrow escapes but it is not worth while to tell you them now. I will wait until I get home...if my life is spared to see it.*

Family service members were rarely spared, and it was a tragic reality of the war that multiple family members died, sometimes destroying whole families. When John heard an unconfirmed report that his younger brother, Jim, was killed at Chancellorsville on May 3, 1863, he reassured his mother that such reports were suspicious. His brother could have been taken prisoner, injured or even missing in action. Why, even John was thought dead by his company on at least one occasion. Unfortunately, his hopes were in vain.

A week later, his mother wrote him with great sadness that she received confirmation of James's death. After a visit to his late brother's regiment, John wrote back. "I went to see the Orderly Sergeant of James' company and he told me all the particulars of James' death...he [James] was hit with a shell or solid shot. It cut one of his legs off and the calf of his other leg and he died while the doctors were at work on him." It was likely a hideous and excruciatingly painful death. John must have suspected that the knowledge of his brother's death would unnerve his mother, but he also knew that she would want to know how her son died.

Thomas D. Marbaker in his *History of the Eleventh New Jersey Volunteers* mentioned James's death. He was killed, he wrote, by a cannonball that ricocheted through his regiment, killing several and maiming several more of his comrades.

Despite common belief, most soldiers did not die from amputations; rather, they were saved by them. More than 110,000 Union troops were killed in action during the war, but more than 224,000 died from disease. For a young boy so anxious to go to war, James would have learned quickly that war was not as exciting as he had imagined. John wrote home that James had talked of desertion, but instead, the youngest Hamilton son chose to fight and died valiantly at Chancellorsville, where the Union casualties totaled 17,000 including 1,600 known dead.

Just one month after Chancellorsville, John's unit was assigned to artillery at the Battle of Gettysburg. His mother, having just lost one son and worried about her wounded husband convalescing in an army hospital, must have been racked with anxiety. She did not hear from John for a month after the battle, but we can imagine that she read carefully the mortality and casualty lists from the battle that were posted daily in New Brunswick and was relieved to see John's name missing from the list.

"I suppose you have heard of the Battle of Gettysburg," John wrote anticlimactically two months later. "I am all right," he wrote to his relieved mother, "but it was a hot place especially for Artillery. It was the heaviest artillery fights of the war."

On July 2, 1863, according to the after-action report submitted by its commander, the First Artillery was positioned near what is now known as Wheatfield Road, close to a peach orchard, where it was pummeled with heavy fire and forced to retreat toward Cemetery Ridge.

"We lost two men killed and six men wounded. One of the men killed was hit right alongside of me…our gun carriage and wheels were pretty well marked with musket balls…I did not get touched," John added.

The next day, July 3, Lieutenant Parsons, commanding the battery in Hexamer's absence due to illness, wrote in his after-action report that the battery was placed farther south of the cemetery, while the enemy's infantry advanced rapidly against Cemetery Ridge. The Confederate's advance became known as Pickett's Charge. In three days, there were more than 51,000 casualties, 23,052 from the Union and 28,063 from the Confederacy.

At Gettysburg, guns and gunners stand ready on July 3, 1863. *Library of Congress.*

"On the 4th," John wrote, "we stood by our guns all day and it rained hard nearly all the day but there was no fighting…It was the worst 4th of July I ever experienced for there were so many dead on the field and they smelled awful."

After Gettysburg, John stayed on the move. Older brother Aleck, whose regiment occupied middle Tennessee, stayed in that state through August 1863 in relative safety. Meanwhile, John's father, who was injured in May 1862, was sent to a convalescing camp at the bottom of Shuter's Hill, an old eighteenth-century plantation in Alexandria, Virginia, to recuperate. He had been there sixty-one days when the surgeon on November 17, 1862, found him "incapable of performing the duties of a soldier," according to his certificate of disability for discharge on record at the National Archives. It appears that the fall or trampling that Alexander experienced, and not the gunshot wound, incapacitated him. He was discharged on November 29, 1862, and traveled back home to New Brunswick, where his health continued to spiral downward.

By early January, the family was urging John to try and obtain a furlough for a visit home to see his ailing father. It was impossible. No furloughs were being given. "I have tried all I know how to get home to see him," he wrote, "and it is all I can do without deserting and I guess he would not want to see me do anything like that nor would you."

He also brought his harried mother words of relief. "We may not see another battle before my time is out, but if we do, I will try and dodge the balls as I have sometimes done before. You may laugh at the idea, but I am satisfied that if I have never done any dodging, I would be a head shorter than I am now."

John's attempt at comic relief disguised his anxiety and concern for his father. He knew from his sister's pleas for him to obtain a furlough that his father was much worse, probably near death. His frustration at not being able to obtain a pass conjured memories of the last time he saw his father, leaving him behind to hobble along on a self-made crutch, while he was ordered to rejoin his regiment.

The word from home came a few days later. John's father, Alexander, the oldest man in his company, had died of the wounds he received at Fair Oaks, probably the result of massive internal injuries. Recounting to his mother the last time he saw his injured father, John wrote, "The next morning we moved again and I kept with him as long as I could. He could not get along very fast so we got behind and when our rear guard came along, they made me leave him and hurry ahead and join my regiment so I had to shake hands with him and leave him in the rear."

It was a touching farewell. John did not know that his parting backward glimpse of his father that day would be his last image of him, burned on his mind for the rest of his life.

West Point, Virginia[1]
May the 8th, 1862

Dear Mother:

We have met the enemy at last. We left Shipping Point and with 2 gun boats came up the river to here and after the gun boats shelled the woods, we landed as soon as the Division were on shore. We advanced towards the woods. Some of the New York and Pennsylvania regiments went in first and they got cut up pretty bad. By the time we got in the Rebs had commenced to retreat and we just had a chance to exchange a few shots with them when we were ordered not to follow them any farther.

I believe there were 6 wounded in our regiment. Some of them were mortal as most of them were buckshot wounds. None of the Brunswick

Boys were wounded. The New York Boys lost pretty heavy. 7 of them lying in one place so close together that had they been alive they could have touched one another and they were scattered through the woods pretty thick so I guess they got the worst of it. I saw plenty of dead Rebs but not so many as the boys in blue. I guess our Captain is a coward for he did not come in the woods with us.

I have heard from Father since and I send you his letter in this. We are in camp outside of the woods now and there is no sign of the enemy.

I will write again as soon as I can. I have not heard from you in over 2 weeks.

My love to all the family and enquiring friends.

From your son,
John

1. West Point is located at the confluence of the Mattapony and Pamunkey Rivers, approximately thirty-five miles east of Richmond. William Franklin's division of Federals attacked Confederate troops near here on May 7.

Gaines Mill, Virginia
June the 6th, 1862

Dear Mother,

I take this opportunity of informing you that I have a whole skin yet and have not been in any very dangerous place since I wrote you last. We have moved camp since I wrote you last but are no [closer to] *Richmond than we were before. There was a battle fought on Fryday*[1] *at Fair Oaks only 3 miles. We had a side view of it and expected to have a hand in it as we were under arms and had 20 extra rounds of cartridges in our pockets and I was a little disappointed when I found we were not agoing.*

We were on picket the other day only 200 yards from them but are not allowed to fire at them. They throw a shell at us once in a while but our batterys are watching them all the time and as soon as they fire a shell at us, our batterys open on them and make them skedaddle in short order. The other day there were about 100 of us at the edge of the woods looking at the Rebs when all at once we saw a flash of a cannon on the hill they were on and you had ought to see the men scatter. I saw at once that they were not firing at us. They were firing at a battery of ours about a quarter of a mile from us, but they only fired 4 shots for our battery opened on them and made the dirt fly so thick around their heads that they left as hard as their horses could carry them.

I send you 15 dollars this time as I want to keep the rest for pocket money. If anything happens to me, I will let you know. Remember me to all

From your absent son,
John

1. The battle, also known as Seven Pines, actually took place on Sunday, June 1. The Confederate commander, Joseph E. Johnston, was wounded and replaced by Jefferson Davis with Robert E. Lee, who promptly initiated plans to drive the Union army from Richmond.

Camp near Harrison Landing, Virginia
July 18th, 1862

Dear Sister,

You see by the head of this letter that we have changed our quarters again. Since I wrote you or mother last we have had a hard time of it. On the 26th of June we were drove out of our camp 3 times by shell from the Rebel batterys and the 3rd time we stayed out and went in camp in the woods.

That night their was awful fighting all night in front of General Porters' Corps on the right of the Army and the next morning he was drove to Gaines Hill and there he made a stand.[1] *And about noon the Rebs attacked him and in a short time after the fight began, an adjutant came to our General and ordered us to go and help Porter. We started and had not got far before we met another adjutant with his hat gone and he gave us orders to hurry to the front. So we started on a run and kept it up for 2 miles and then we were close to the front and we formed a line of battle and advanced into the woods.*

There was 2 lines of our men in the woods and when we came in they stopped firing and lay down and we went over them at a double quick and a cheer and drove the Rebs about 50 yards. And then they gave it to us so thick that we stopped and commenced firing. We were about 30 yards apart and the smoke was so thick that we could not see each other. But if we stooped down we could see their legs. Their was a Zoave Regiment on the right of us and our company came on a line with them. I was in among them and from where I was I could see what I was firing at and was so interested in my shooting that I did not think of danger.

Our Brigade was relieved at about 4 o'clock in the afternoon but I was with this Zoave regiment and we advanced about 50 yards farther. So I did not know that our brigade had gone out. So I stayed in until dark. The nearest I came to getting hit that I know was once I went to take aim from behind a tree and a ball hit the tree within an inch of my face. The bark hit me in the eyes and I thought at the time that I was wounded but I came out all right. Only I had used cartridges all up, but 5 rounds and when I went in I have 60 rounds.

When I came out I had to come through a deep mud hole and my shoes were untied and they stuck in the mud and I lost them but I had not got outside of the woods far before I came to some knapsacks and some shoes were handing to them. And I stopped and got a pair for myself and a pair for Furlong as I knew he wanted a pair.

While I was getting them our Calvary went past me on a charge and I sat down on one of the knapsacks and commenced putting on my shoes and watching the cavalry charge, but they did not go far. For as soon as they came near the wood, there was a line of Rebels raised up in the woods and gave them an awful volley of musket balls and emptyed nearly half of their saddles and wounded and killed nearly half of their horses. The wounded horses turned and came back like mad with their heads up in the air. Most of them were wounded in the head and they could not see where they were going. I saw them coming towards me so I jumped into a lot of ivy bushes to get clear of them but they came right over me and knocked me down and trampled me in the mud. But they went over me so quick and the bushes were so thick that they did not hurt me much. I had one shoe on when they run over me and the other 3 under my arm and they trampled the shoes and my cap so far in the mud that I could not find them and as it was getting dark I thought I had better get out of that and find my regiment. I found the regiment in the old camp. It was about 9 o'clock at night when I found them and they had been there since about half past 5 o'clock in the afternoon.

Our company thought I was killed. I had no trouble to get a cap in the company but I could not get any shoes. Our company lost 4 killed and 10 wounded. I don't know how many the regiment lost. The 4th Regiment were nearly all killed or taken prisoners with their colors. The 2nd Regiment lost their Colonel and colors. Our Regiment came out the best of any of the Brigade.

I must tell you about our Colonel. He was very sick and lying in his tent and when we left camp to go to the battle, he made his servant open the front of the tent so he could see us pass. He was so sick that he could hardly sit up but when he heard the fighting going on so hard, he got so uneasy that he could not stay in his tent. So he ordered an ambulance to take him to the field but the ambulance did not go fast enough for him so he got out and got on his horse, a splendid big black horse and came up and into the woods where the Regiment was. And he looked like a wild man. Some of the officers tryed to make him go back but he stayed until the regiment went out and he has been with the regiment ever since although he is not well.

We left our camp the next day[2] *and with the army started towards James River. The second night we were on the march, Father came into our camp looking after me. He was wounded in the thigh and was walking with a stick. He could not get in an ambulance as they were all full. He got wounded at Fair Oaks. He was in the battle of Williamsburg*[3] *but came out of that with a whole skin. He slept with me that night and we were talking together until about 12 o'clock when I heard the orderly calling my name and I found I had to leave my comfortable bed and go and guard an old bridge as the Rebs were trying to burn it down. There were about 400 of us went and it was raining and as dark as it could be when we got there. We drove some rebel cavalry away and then stood there in the rain until daylight.*

When I got back to camp Father had a good breakfast for me. When I left him in the middle of the night he shook hands with me and says, "If they kill you, John, I will give them the devil." So he was glad to see me come back again in the morning all right. We had just time to eat our breakfast when we were ordered to fall in and break camp.

Father could not walk fast enough to keep up to us and they would not let me stay behind with him. So we soon got a head of him and I have not seen him since. On the evening of the 1st of July[4] *General Kearney was in a hard fight with his Corps and was getting the worse of it. And he sent for his old brigade. We were in the woods at the line and had just commenced to cook our coffee when the order came that our old general wanted us to help him.*

The coffee was thrown away and our knapsacks, blankets and everything but our canteens and haversacks. And we ran about 2 miles through the woods. The artillery of the enemy were engaged with Kearney's Division. And their shell came bouncing through the woods past us. Some of the men were killed by them. We advanced up within 20 feet of Kearney's line of battle and gave him 9 cheers. And when the noise of our cheering had ceased we could hear the Rebs getting away from our front. We could hear them giving orders to the artillery. I suppose they thought that a whole corps had come to support Kearney. For when we cheered, Kearney's men cheered us and it sounded as if there were a lot of fresh troops just arrived. And we were glad to hear their artillery getting away at a dead run.

The next morning we got into Malvern Hill about 3 o'clock with Kearney's Division and we were the last troops that came in from the retreat. It was so dark that last night of the retreat that we had to hold on to each others haversacks to keep from getting lost and we were so close to the enemy that we were not allowed to speak above a whisper. When we got on Malvern Hill, it was not daylight yet so we lay down on our arms until we were woke up by shell bursting around our heads. And it was splendid sight that we saw for we were about the center of Malvern Hill and could see the whole army. They lay along the brow of the hill and one artillery had a position on the top. There were plenty of artillery and our large siege guns were also in position. The gunboats in the James River were throwing shells over our heads at the Rebs who were just advancing.[5]

But we had not long to look at this for we were ordered to fall back with Kearney's Division to Harrison's Landing. As we were the last ones that came in on the retreat and covered it and we were not sorry to get off of Malvern Hill for the shell from the rebel battery were bursting around our heads uncomfortably close. When we got down to the river it was about 10 o'clock in the morning.

We went into a large wheat field and it commenced to rain as hard as it could pour down. We went into camp in the field and as none of us had anything to eat a lot of us started down to the edge of the river where we saw a large pile of cracker boxes. When we got there, the guard told us to help ourselves and I filled my shirt around my waist and all my pockets and hat besides putting a good share inside of my ribs. By the time I got back to camp I was as wet as a drowned rat and the crackers were all soft but the men were all crazy to get one notwithstanding. I gave them all away but enough for me and Furlong to eat.

I had not been in camp half an hour before we were ordered to move again about 2 miles farther up the River. We had crossed a creek and the water was over waist deep. We held our cartridge boxes over our heads and waded through but we might as well fall we were wet through before we came to it. On the 6th of July I was detailed among some more the Regiment to fix and road and while I was working on the road Aleck came across me. He was looking after me and came upon me by accident. I went with him to his camp which was only about 100 yards from where we were working and I stayed and took dinner with him. He looks well. He is orderly sergeant of his company.

I received your letter to day and was glad to hear that Father was home. I have looked in nearly every hospital in the Army and I had come to the conclusion that he was either dead or taken prisoner which is the next thing to it.

I saw Aleck again the other day. His company, with another of the 8th regulars, are at McClellans headquarters doing provost duty. They are kept very strict and not allowed to go out of camp without a pass for half an hour. I have been away from camp nearly every day for the last week down to the landing and when I came back nights, the lieutenant would ask me where I had been and I would tell him and he said all right only dont go away from camp when you are detailed for any duty.

I am sorry to hear that mother is sick and hope ere this reaches you she will be all well. Tell her to send me a pocket handkerchief in the next paper she sends me for it is awful hot here and the sweat runs into our eyes and nearly blinds us. We are having pretty hard duty now as we have to work on the trenches and every 3rd day we have to go on picket but I guess we will soon have the trenches finished.

I am sorry that James has enlisted and hope Father can get him out again.
Give my love to Mother and the rest.

From your afectionate brother,
John P. Hamilton

1. General Lee began his campaign to drive the Federals from the gates of Richmond, called the Seven Days' Battles, on June 26, attacking Fitz John Porter's corps at Mechanicsville, north of the Confederate capital. On June 27, Lee attacked him again at Gaines's Mill.
2. On June 28, General McClellan ordered the army to change its base to Harrison's Landing on the James River south of Richmond.
3. Battle earlier in the campaign on May 5, 1862.
4. Actually June 30, the Battle of Frayser's Farm or Glendale.
5. John is describing the action known as the Battle of Malvern Hill, July 1, 1862.

Chapter 8
Brothers in Arms

I met Aleck on the road…he had the fever and ague, so he could not keep up to his company. The Sergeant was carrying his rifle for him. I slept with him that night and the next day in the afternoon I caught up with my regiment.
–September 20, 1862, camp on South Mountain, Maryland

The first Hamilton to join the Union fight was brother Aleck. Two years older than John and the first boy in the family, Aleck exhibited an independent streak. He chose not to move with the family from Massachusetts to New Jersey in the 1850s but instead traveled west to Eel, Indiana, a sleepy town situated on the Eel River with a population of less than three thousand in 1860. Just outside the county seat of Logansport, Aleck worked as a cabinetmaker's apprentice along with another young man.

John had not seen Aleck in some years due to the distance separating them, John living in New Jersey and Aleck in Indiana. When John learned that Aleck had enlisted, he wrote to his mother in August 1861, "Tell Aleck I would like to see him [when you write]. I suppose he is a six-footer now, but I think I would know him."

A true six-footer, with dark hair and the family's gray eyes, according to his veteran medical records, Aleck turned nineteen on April 2, 1861, and was one of the first to answer President Lincoln's call for men. He enlisted less than a week later at the Fourth and Market Streets recruiting office in Logansport, and his was the first company to be mustered into the army,

Company K, Ninth Indiana Infantry. He was commissioned as second lieutenant to the company under Captain Dudley H. Chase.

With only a month of training in Indianapolis, the regiment was ordered to Grafton in western Virginia (present-day West Virginia) in late May and attached to Colonel Benjamin F. Kelly's command, the First Virginia Infantry. Aleck's company quickly saw action in June at Philippi and then participated in the Western Virginia Campaign in July at Laurel Hill, Rich Mountain and Corrick's Ford, the first campaigns of the Civil War. At stake was control of the Baltimore & Ohio Railroad, an important regional railroad providing access to the North and South. The conflicts also marked the meteoric rise of General George McClellan, who used the victories and the telegraph to speed the good news to Washington. These Union victories, squashing Confederate movements, were small clashes compared with what was to come, but many Northerners were energized by the victories and believed that the war would end at Manassas, Virginia, in July.

Aleck's three-month stint in the Volunteers ended in early August, and it seems likely (John's letters imply it) that he traveled during his break to New Brunswick to visit his mother, his youngest brother, James, and his sisters. His visit and war stories may have fueled sixteen-year-old James's interest in joining the army. John urged his mother to "tell him [James] if he knows as much as I do about soldiering he wont bother his head about coming out. If he is once sworn into the service, he must do soldiers duty whether he likes it or not."

Several months later, Aleck reenlisted in November 1861 as a private in Company H, First Battalion, Nineteenth Indiana Infantry, at Indianapolis. "I am sorry to hear he enlisted as a private," John wrote to his mother, "for I think he could have got a commission in the Volunteers if he had tried but if he can get a commission in the regular army, it will be better a great deal." It is unclear why Aleck did not seek a commission since there are no known letters that exist to explain it.

As a seasoned veteran, Aleck's first job was as a recruiting officer in Logansport. The recruiting office was presided over by a line officer directly from the front or an experienced soldier recently commissioned. Unlike the beginning of the war, recruits came slowly, he told brother John. By May 1862, Company H had been ordered to Washington, D.C., attached to Brigadier General Samuel D. Sturgis's command, Military District.

It was a fine opportunity for Aleck. General George McClellan, who assumed command of the Army of the Potomac the previous year, established provost marshals and provost guards to keep the peace. The guards' "special and sole" duty was to preserve property and arrest "all

A group of provost guards at the headquarters of the Army of the Potomac at Petersburg, Virginia. *Library of Congress.*

wrong-doers, of whatever regiment or corps they may be." Only men of integrity and character were chosen to be provost guards, and Aleck was now one of them. For his mother, it must have been wonderful news: provost guards did not fight at the front. At least one Hamilton was safe.

At home, James was itching to join the cause and had left his job at the rubber factory store. At his mother's urging, John wrote to him in December 1861: "Mother says that you have got it into your head that you want to get with Aleck in the Army. Don't you do it, Jim, for I think that is enough if we are all in the Army but you and yours had better stay home and go back to your place again or do anything but soldier for you are too young to soldier…it is no easy life, I can assure you."

John's entreaties fell on deaf ears. Mary Ann wrote to him a month later that "James has still got soldiering in his head." A few weeks later, John commiserated with his mother. "I am sorry that James is so unsettled yet and hope he will give up his soldiering notions and go to work again." It must have been frustrating for young James to have watched his father and two older brothers join the war effort, while he sat at home with his sisters and his mother. The "men" of the family—or so it seemed—were having all the excitement, all except James.

In February 1862, John was elated to hear that James had gone back to work. It was a short reprieve. In June, against the wishes of his family, the only Hamilton son left in New Brunswick enlisted in Company F, Eleventh New Jersey Regiment, as a private. He was mustered into service at Camp Perrine in Trenton, New Jersey, for three years. The regiment left New Jersey for Washington on August 25, 1862. Mary Ann was devastated to give her last son to the cause.

By July of the same year, Aleck's company was on the move, with McClellan following him to his headquarters at Berkeley Plantation in Charles City, near Harrison's Landing in Virginia. John also was near the landing at a camp. It had been years since the two were together: "On the 6th of July I was detailed…to fix the road and while I was working…Aleck came across me…by accident. I went with him to his camp which was only about 100 yards from where we were working and I stayed and took dinner with him. He looks well."

By this time, Aleck had been made an orderly sergeant for his company. John again ran into Aleck a few days later: "His company with another…are at McClellan's Headquarters doing provost duty. They are kept very strict and not allowed to go out of camp without a pass for half an hour."

The brothers spent as much time as they could catching up for lost years: "I have been away from camp nearly every night for the last week [with Aleck]…and when I came back nights, the lieutenant would ask me where I have been and I would tell him [with my brother] and he said, 'All right, only don't go away from camp when you are detailed for any duty.'"

When John's regiment moved in October 1862, the brothers were separated again. John reminded his mother that although he had not seen Aleck lately, "he is all right. For you know he belongs…to the provost guard and they don't have to go in a fight." That would change in November when McClellan was relieved of his command.

In the meantime, James's regiment, with a full complement of men, was ordered to Washington, D.C., at the end of August 1862. They camped at Georgetown awaiting orders. Ironically, John was across the river in Alexandria at the end of August for a short time before leaving for Bull Run and what would be the Second Battle of Bull Run.

When John discovered that James's regiment was camped at Georgetown, he decided to visit him. Unknown to John, James's regiment was at half strength due to a serious outbreak of measles that ran through the camp.

The chain bridge just below Little Falls in Georgetown was close to James's camp. The bridge provided a crossing between Virginia and Georgetown. *Library of Congress.*

"So I went ahead in the night and the next morning I got in Georgetown and found that his Regiment was in camp at the Chain Bridge. There were some green troops guarding the bridge…they showed me the camp on the other side of the bridge, but they would not let me cross."

John traveled six miles out of his way with a knapsack on his back to see a brother he had not seen in two years only to be thwarted at the last moment. He did not tell his mother what he said to the guard at the bridge, only that he was impolite and let them know what he thought. Understandably, he was frustrated and angry. All was not lost, however. As he hurried to catch his own company, he met Aleck on the road with another sergeant: "[Aleck] has the fever and ague…the Sergeant was carrying his rifle for him. I slept with him that night and the next day in the afternoon I caught up to my Regiment."

Finally, John reunited with James one night in December 1862 before the Battle at Fredericksburg, Virginia. Both John and James's regiments were scheduled to fight at Fredericksburg, one of the North's costliest defeats.

After fighting in and surviving his first major battle, James was disenchanted, homesick and ready to desert. He confided in his brother John, who cautioned him on the perils of desertion. Some deserters were welcomed back with open arms by battle-wearied officers; others were shot as an example.

Desertion was a common occurrence. Estimates put Union deserters at 200,000 and Confederate at 104,000. Homesickness, like James experienced, was one cause. Other soldiers were sick of poor food, unhealthy camp conditions, boredom or lack of confidence in their commanders. Some "deserted" on a self-granted furlough to return weeks later.

Worried about James, John urged his mother to ask his father to write to him. Near White Oak Church, Virginia, in February 1863, John again visited a homesick James and expressed concern to his mother that his brother was thinking of desertion: "Tell Father to write to Jim for he has got a notion he wants to come home and, of course, he cannot without getting into trouble and if Father writes him a good letter, it may do him good."

Aleck's military life was changing, too. With McClellan's loss of command at the end of 1862, the Nineteenth Indiana Infantry Provost Guards were disbanded, and its soldiers were absorbed into the regular ranks. On April 2, 1863, John received a letter from Aleck noting that it was his older brother's birthday. That same month, Aleck's regiment was ordered to advance on Murfreesboro in Tennessee. Aleck's regiment would perform occupation duties in Tennessee through August 1863.

In the same letter of April 1863, John reported to his mother that he saw James, who "looks well," and added that the boots she sent him "fit him." Months later, as John's company prepared for the battle at Fredericksburg, John again saw James, who "is under the same orders that we are."

The fight at Fredericksburg occurred December 11–25, 1862, and was hard fought. More than 172,000 men under the principal commands of Major General Ambrose E. Burnside for the Union and General Robert E. Lee for the Confederacy met in the one of the largest but one-sided battles of the war. Lee entrenched his army on the heights west of the town; Burnside mounted a series of futile frontal attacks on Prospect Hill and Marye's Heights, where the advancing soldiers were picked off by the bucketful. The result was staggering casualties for the Union, more than twice the number of the Confederate army. On December 15, Burnside called off the offensive and retreated.

When the smoke of the battle cleared, John waited to hear from James and his safe conduct from the battle. He neither saw nor heard from him

Major General Alfred T.A. Torbert, one of John's commanding officers, was cited several times in John's letters home for his bravery and leadership. *Library of Congress.*

but was not overly concerned. "His regiment has been engaged but I do not know where his regiment is now," he wrote to his mother, adding with no assurance that "I don't know whether he was hurt or not, but I don't suppose he was or else I would have heard it for bad news always travels fast."

By early January 1863, John had good and bad news for the family. Writing his sister Mary Jane, he reported that he had seen James. "He is all right only he has got it into his head to try and go home when he gets paid. Furlough or no furlough it will take a smart man to go home without the proper papers and I told him if he tried it, he would be shure caught and it might go hard with him. I told him he had better make up his mind to stay until his time was out and then he would be home as soon as I would."

For the young boy so excited by the prospect of war and eager to leave the security of home, it was a complete turnaround. The reality of war, the horrid deaths of friends and the stink and heat of artillery fire led to a fierce desire to run from the battlefield, and yet courage and his brother's advice prevailed. James stayed.

Camp on South Mountain, Maryland
Sept the 20th, 1862

Dear Mother:

You see by the heading of this letter I have moved camp again.[1] *We left the Seminary the next night after I wrote you last and crossed Long Bridge to Washington and I found that we were a going through Georgetown into Maryland and as I heard that the 11th New Jersey were somewhere about Georgetown, I thought I would go ahead and see James.*

So I went ahead in the night and the next morning I got in Georgetown and found that his regiment was in camp at the Chain Bridge so I went there and there were some green troops guarding the bridge. I asked them if they knew where the 11th were in camped and they showed me the camp on the other side of the bridge, but they would not let me cross the bridge.

So after coming over 6 miles out of my way with a knapsack on my back to see a brother that I had not saw for 2 years I had to turn back again without seeing him although I was so near his regiment I could almost throw a stone to them. If the men who guarded the bridge were old soldiers, they would have let me cross, but they were green troops.[2] *When I found they would not let me cross over, I told them what I thought of them and I was not very polite about it either.*

When I got back to Georgetown I found that the regiment had gone through 3 hours and consequently I was some miles behind them so I started after them in the afternoon. I met Aleck on the road with another Sergeant of his regiment. He had the fever and ague, so he could not keep up to his company. The Sergeant was carrying his rifle for him. I slept with them that night and the next day in the afternoon I caught up to my regiment.

My captain asked me where I had been. I expected he would punish me, but when I told him I had been looking after my brother, he said it was all right.

The next day we run against the Rebs. They were strongly posted in a pass in the mountain called Crampton Pass.[3] *Our division moved up in front of them. Some of the New York regiments drove their skirmishes in and got a position at about 300 yards from the foot of the mountain behind a rail fence and we formed our line about half a mile behind them and advanced across the open fields under an awful artillery fire from the Rebs on the mountain. But only 3 of their shells done any damage to the regiment and I believe they killed 6 and wounded 9 or 10 men.*

As soon as we got to the rail fence where the New York Regiments were, we lay down behind them. We had not lain there but a few minutes before General Slocum came to Colonel Torbert and told him that the Rebs must [be] *driven from that Pass before dark. Colonel Torbert told him he thought they would not stand a charge and he believed a charge would clear them out. As soon as Slocum rode away, we were ordered to fix bayonets and get up and move forward. Between us and the foot of the mountain, there was a corn field and the other side of that there was a stone wall behind which the Rebels were laying besides another line of them half way up the mountain and the main body was on top in the pass. As soon as we started for the mountain, the Rebs heard us, but the corn was so high they could not see us, but they opened their fire and the way their bullets cut the tops off the corn, I thought there would be a poor chance of getting through with a whole skin.*

Our whole line gave a yell and started through the corn at a run and were over the stone wall among the Rebs before they knew hardly what was the matter. They did not show much fight when we were among them but threw their arms down and went to the rear and as soon as we formed our line we started up the hill driving some of the Rebs before us. We had not got far before the second line of Rebs opened a volley on us and I got hit in the head and knocked down but was up again in a minute and feeling of my head not feeling any blood, I went ahead again. The Rebs had broke and were running up the mountain as fast they could and we were gaining on them and taking them prisoners by the dozens.

A lot of us were running after a squad of the Rebs that were trying to get away by going more to the left of us. When just as were passing a tree that had blown down with the roots sticking up in the air, a rebel stepped from behind the roots and fired his rifle in my face. So close was he that I could not see for some minutes. When I got my eyes open I found some of our fellows had taken him prisoner. If he had been in front of me when I got my eyes open I do believe I would have shot him for he had no right to shoot when he saw he had no chance to get away. In fact some of our men were between him and his regiment so he must [have] *been so excited he did not know what he was doing.*

When we got to the top of the Pass some of the Rebs had made a stand there but when they saw that we did not stop, they broke and part of them threw down their arms and surrendered. We followed the rest down the other side of the mountain about a mile and a half and then it was dark. We could not see, so we were ordered back again to the Pass. We stayed there that night.

I examined my head and found a lump about as large as my fist and part of my hat gone. I think that a ball struck a stone in front of me and flattened and struck me flat on the head or else it was a stone. I don't know which.

An order was read to us the next day giving us great praise for acting so well the day before. I took 2 prisoners and when I was bringing them in I found that one of them was acquainted with Mat Severance. He knew him in Savannah. He says that Mat is in the Washington Artillery or was the last he heard of him.

That night we left the Pass and moved towards Sharpsburg and the next morning we went into Antietam. Colonel Torbert had his horse shot out from under him just as we were going in to take our position. We had to take our position under a galling fire of both artillery and infantry. But when we got our position, we lay down and then it was not so bad as the enemy could not see us. Jim Furlong got hit on the shoulder by a piece of shell, but not bad. I suppose he will get over it in 4 or 5 weeks. The Rebels shelled us all day and once in a while they would wing someone in the line. But our batterys replied to them so often that they could not shoot as nice as they otherwise would.

That night I was on the skirmish line about 50 yards from the Rebs and we had to lay flat on our faces or else we would draw a shot at us. Where I laid I could count 6 dead Rebels almost in reach of me and as the day before had been so hot, they smelt awful, but we had to stand it as it was almost death to move and besides it would be hard to find a place on that field that was not pretty well covered with dead. It is the worse sight I have saw yet.

Yesterday morning we found that the Rebs had retreated[4] *and we started after them. We passed across the battle field and it was an awful sight to see the dead. Most of them were Rebels and they had turned as black as n** and swelled so large, they looked as if they would burst.*

We are now in camp and the Rebs have retreated over the Potomac.

Give my love to all.

From your affectionate son,
John

1. The Army of the Potomac, under General McClellan, was pursuing the Confederate Army of Northern Virginia as it invaded Maryland.
2. Green troops were men who were new to the job—in this case, picket duty.
3. Actually, Crampton's Pass is in Maryland. General Franklin's left wing of the Sixth Corps attacked the Confederates defending the pass on September 14, 1862.
4. After the Battle of Antietam or Sharpsburg on September 17, 1862, known as the bloodiest single day of the war, General Lee's Confederate Army of Northern Virginia retreated across the Potomac into Virginia on the night of September 18–19.

Chapter 9
The Boys

None of the Brunswick boys were wounded.
–May 8, 1862, West Point, Virginia

As diverse in age and employment at they were, the Brunswick Boys shared a bond of friendship made stronger by their experiences in the war. Some, like "little" Martin Connelly, only seventeen years old in 1861, distinguished themselves with heroic feats of bravery on the battlefield; others, like John, stood steadfast at their post despite heavy fire, exhausting heat and dead comrades. There were still others, like Tom Corrigan, who spent time in the infamous Confederate prison at Andersonville, where, in the fourteen months of its existence beginning in 1864, some forty-five thousand Union soldiers were confined, thirteen thousand of whom died from disease, malnutrition, overcrowding, exposure and a woeful lack of basic sanitation.

John knew all the Boys before the war through their employment, family connections or as friends who socialized together. The war forged them into men who would never forget their experiences and the bonds that tied them together.

An immigrant to New Brunswick from England, twenty-five-year-old Charles Banks worked as a porter in a store in 1861. He boarded with the Lindley family, who also had emigrated from England. Enlisting at the start of the war as a private in Company K, Third New Jersey Infantry Regiment, Charlie Banks was one of the first familiar faces John met after enlistment.

Their meeting was memorialized in one of his first letters home. "I saw Charlie Banks and he looks well, only a little sun burnt."

Just two weeks later, John reunited with twenty-six-year-old Julius (Jule) Meyers, a friend and boatman and the oldest child and sole support of his widowed mother and six brothers and sisters in New Brunswick. Jule had joined Company F, First New Jersey Infantry, in June 1861.

To compensate for the lost revenue stream from his boatman wages, the City of New Brunswick paid subsistence pay to his dependent mother in quarterly payments of eighteen dollars to help defray support for the Meyers children. Certainly, Jule sent part or all of his paycheck home, as did John, who sent his pay regularly to his mother.

John saw Jule after the First Battle of Bull Run, when the soldiers were scavenging the field searching for weapons, boots, jackets and other salvageable items they might use. "Some of the boys," he told his mother, "found several things on the battle field. Jule Meyers found a carbine."

John's regiment was joined by ten other men from New Brunswick. Among them was David Skillman, twenty-two, a machinist at the shoe factory, who arrived with John Tyler Lewis, eighteen, who also worked at the rubber factory. Both boys were good friends with John, and both joined Company G, Fourth New Jersey Infantry, in August 1861.

Another Brunswick Boy and friend to John's sister Mary Jane was Isaac (Ike) DeForrest, who enlisted in May 1861 as a private in Company K, Second New Jersey Infantry Regiment. Ike was discharged with a disability in Virginia in February 1863 and returned home.

It was comforting to have familiar faces and friends about, even more so on the battle field. At Second Bull Run near Manassas in August 1862, Thomas Corrigan, a twenty-year-old apprentice carpenter from New Brunswick, was with John. Corrigan was a private with the Eighth New Jersey Regiment. The boys were pressed by the Rebel artillery, and their brigade advanced ahead of them, while John and Tom stayed behind to help a Company A man who was wounded in the leg. They were caught in the Union's disorganized retreat, a rout that embraced man and beast:

> *I had caught a horse and was helping the wounded man…when two pieces of…artillery passed me. Tom Corrigan was with me. We saw our chance was small so we left the wounded man as we could not get away with him. I found a creek with elder bushes growing on each side so thick we could not be seen…We jumped into the creek. I was ahead and Tom was behind me…We thought we would go up to the place where we left our*

> *knapsacks...but the Rebels were already there so we struck into the woods towards the railroad.*

Exhausted, John collapsed but then struggled forward, the fear of capture spurring him on. Two-thirds of John's brigade were lost that day. Most were taken prisoners. Tom was wounded in the hand and neck, but he survived, only to be taken prisoner in 1864 and sent to the infamous Andersonville Prison in Georgia, where he spent nine months before being released. Tom was one of the few to survive the ordeal of the prison.

The war changed the Boys in all respects, not the least their physical appearance. Some lost weight through poor diet or disease; many lost limbs, and some aged beyond their years. George Fouratt, John's brother-in-law's cousin, who also worked with John in the rubber factory, was no exception. "I went the other day to see George," John wrote his mother. "I hardly knew him he has so much whiskers. He is in good health but he has got enough of the Army already."

Fouratt and Bill Furlong, Jim Furlong's brother, joined the army together in July 1862 and served in Company F, Twenty-eighth New Jersey Regiment Infantry.

Benjamin L. Moffett, another New Brunswick friend, joined Company E, First New Jersey Regiment Infantry, in early 1861 and was made a corporal by May and then promoted to sergeant. Receiving a commission for second lieutenant in March 1863, Moffitt, newly married, was granted a furlough to go home. John asked him to take his broken watch so his mother could have it repaired.

When he returned to camp, John commented that Ben had been given a "soft place" in charge of an ambulance corp. "He has a horse to ride and he will not be apt to see much fighting," he told his mother. Ironically, Moffitt was critically wounded in action at the Battle of the Wilderness in Virginia on May 8, 1864, and died the following day.

Death was a close companion to all the boys. They witnessed the men around them fall and, like all soldiers, grew hard to the reality, even when it affected close friends and family. A denial of emotion is a psychological coping mechanism for survival, often employed by soldiers in war. When John, for example, heard a company report of a death of someone close to him, he was unconvinced at first. He could have been captured, he reasoned, missing or misreported as dead. "I remember at the Battle of Gains Mills," he wrote his mother, "two men of Capt. Fouratt's company were supposed to have been killed and were marked dark on the company books and they both turned up again. One of them was Peter McGovern."

Captain Jarvis Wanser of the Fourteenth New Jersey Volunteers was a Brunswick Boy well known to John. *New Jersey State Archives, Department of State.*

Irish-born McGovern was another married Brunswick Boy, who joined the First New Jersey Infantry, Company F, as a private in 1861. Another changed man was Jarvis Wanser, who joined Company H, Fourteenth New Jersey Regiment, in 1862. At twenty-two, Jarvis worked as a bartender in his father's saloon. Married since 1858, he was promoted to sergeant a few months after he joined. Promoted again to second lieutenant in May 1864, then to first lieutenant, he made captain before he was mustered out in June 1865.

Army life agreed with Jarvis. When John reunited with him at camp near Rappahannock Station in August 1863, Jarvis "was fat and hearty," and the Brunswick Boys had a fine reunion together. "We are on picket duty here but we have a good time," John reported.

Another close friend, Sailor Bill, along with William Furlong and George Fouratt, joined Company F, Twenty-eighth New Jersey Regiment Infantry, in September 1862. "Sailor Bill" was an affectionate nickname for a New Brunswick companion whom John never identified in his letters with a last name. His unit was researched through regimental lists to discover his full name. Through a process of elimination, it is highly probable that Sailor Bill was William Stroud.

The sobriquet "Sailor Bill" referred to a bawdy drinking song about a sailor named Bill. It is likely that Stroud was a drinking companion of the boys in New Brunswick, thus earning the affectionate pet name. When war was first declared, Sailor Bill stayed home. He wrote to John shortly after the latter enlisted in the volunteers, stating that he would join him if his company needed more men. "I wrote to him [Sailor Bill] and told him that we did not want more but I did not get any answer so I suppose he has backed out of it."

To the contrary, Stroud joined with his friends Furlong and Fouratt when the new regiment organized in Freehold, New Jersey. John saw Sailor Bill with regularity since his regiment, like John's, was stationed in Washington, D.C., for a time. Eventually, both Sailor Bill and John's regiments participated in the bitter and bloody fighting at the Battle of Fredericksburg on December 18, 1862, and later the disastrous Union campaign at Chancellorsville in April and May 1863. Stroud received a brevet promotion to sergeant for meritorious service.

There is little doubt that John knew Sailor Bill intimately and trusted him thoroughly. When Sailor Bill was about to be mustered out of the army and return to New Brunswick, John entrusted him to bring his personal belongings home to his mother.

Sometimes, the most humble and unassuming of the Boys performed the most heroic deeds. Irish-born Martin Connelly, seventeen years old in 1861, worked with John in the rubber factory. He enlisted in Company A, Fifty-seventh New York Infantry Regiment, in September 1861 after the New Jersey regiments were filled. He "use to drill buttons in the factory," John wrote. "He came out here as a private...was promoted to color bearer for bravery and at the Battle of Antietam was wounded in four different places while carrying the flag."

Connelly was promoted to sergeant in January 1863. He "brought the colors out with him" at the Battle of Chancellorsville. He also distinguished himself and was promoted to quartermaster sergeant and then to second lieutenant. John admired his friend's bravery and spunk. "He has made out better than any of the New Brunswick Boys and it is all owing to his bravery for when he enlisted he was a stranger to all of his comrades and officers."

Another button factory connection was John Vroom, a thirty-one-year-old Brunswick boatman and friend of John's who married Julia Stilwell before the start of the war. Sisters Sarah and Julia Stillwell were neighbors to Vroom. The girls worked at the button factory, the same factory where Martin Connolly worked.

John also asked Vroom to visit his mother while Vroom was on furlough in 1864. It was not uncommon for the Brunswick Boys to ask one another, when on furlough, to visit their family members. Many of the Boys, who knew Mrs. Hamilton, gladly visited her to report on John's condition, and he, in turn, trusted them to put a good face on the war and not worry

Captain George M. Stelle of the Eighth New Jersey Volunteers, a Brunswick Boy, knew John through the rubber factory where his father worked. *New Jersey State Archives, Department of State.*

his mother needlessly during his four years of service. Indeed, he trusted Vroom to bring a treasured photograph of Susie, Alice and his mother back to him.

Another connection to the factory was Captain George M. Stelle, Eighth New Jersey Volunteers. George's father, James, worked in the rubber factory, and the Stelle family lived with one of the factory superintendents, Louis Platt. Although John did not mention George specifically in his letters, there was a clear connection between the two men.

Even the Brunswick Boys who were mustered out were not forgotten. Michael Welsh, another rubber factory colleague who worked with John, enlisted in Company F, First New Jersey Regiment, and was mustered out in June 1864. "If you see Mike Welsh," John directed his mother, "ask him why he dont answer my letter." There was no leeway offered among the Brunswick Boys.

Camp near the Seminary, Virginia.
September 1862

Dear Mother,

When I wrote you last we were on the Potomac. We landed at Alexandria and got on the cars [railroad cars] *immediately and went out to Bull Run Bridge.*[1] *Our Brigade orders were to guard the Bridge, to keep the enemy from burning it, but when we got there we heard some firing. So we were ordered to move forward to where the firing was. We had not gone far before we came to the top of a hill and from there we could see what the firing was. It appears one of our batterys was in camp out there and the Rebs had got into their camp by surprise and they had time enough to get away with 2 piece of their battery and the Rebs had turned the other 4 pieces and was firing at them as they were getting away. Our General saw it at a glance and ordered us to throw off our knapsacks and rifle and we started for the Rebs. We thought that it was only some cavalry or guerrillas, but we found out our mistake as you will see.*

As soon as we got pretty near them, they fell back to the other side of the battery camp and dragged the 4 pieces of artillery into an old form {This was near Manassas, and it was one of the forts that the Rebels had built at the first of the war} and pointed them out of the embrasures. Our line advanced pretty near the fort when we saw a line of men to the left of it and we changed our course toward them thus exposing our flank to the fort. And they commenced firing canister at us which told awfully on our line as we went through the artillery camp. The canister struck among the tents and it sounded like throwing a hand full of shot among a lot of newspapers.

After we got through the camp, it got so hot for us we were ordered to stop and lay down. We were about 200 yards from the fort then so we kept the battery nearly silenced. We had not lain there but a few minutes before we saw a regiment of Rebs come out of the woods and lay down in line in front of us about 800 yards from us. We then got orders to fix our bayonets and I thought we were about to charge them and believe we would, but just then we saw a large body of troops moving around our flank to get in rear of us and we were ordered to fall back.

As soon as we commenced moving back the line of Rebs that were in front of us rose up and gave us a volley and came after us at a run and the battery in the fort opened on us again and 3 or 4 other batterys that we had not seen before commenced throwing grape and canister by the wholesale. We saw that if we did not get back to the railroad before the Rebs did, we were cut off and must all be captured as there appeared to be no end to their numbers and our brigade was alone. The Brigade got broke and mixed up but we made a stand for a while. But our General ordered us to get back to the bridge as soon as we could and form a line there and protect it, if possible. In the mean time the Rebs were following us up with their artillery and infantry and sending death into us every minute… [What follows is John's description of his involvement in the Second Battle of Manassas or Bull Run. The Union army under John Pope was soundly defeated.]

The day was very hot and a great many gave out and were taken prisoners. I came very near being taken myself. I stayed behind to help one of Company A men. He was wounded in the leg. While I was helping, the Brigade got about half a mile ahead of me. I had caught a horse and was helping the wounded man on his back when 2 pieces of the Rebel artillery passed me and swung around and commenced firing at the brigade. So they were between me and the brigade. Tom Corrigan was with me. We saw our chance was small so we left the wounded man as we could not get away with him and as good luck would have it, I found a creek with elder bushes growing on each side so thick that we could not be seen. We jumped into the creek. I was ahead and Tom was behind me. We struck Bull Run and crossed it all right and then we thought we would go up to the place where we left our knapsacks and haversacks and get them. But the Rebels were already there so we struck into the woods towards the railroad.

Once I laid down I was so fatigued I thought I would let them take me prisoner, but when I heard them coming through the woods, I thought of Libby Prison[2] *and I got up again and reached the railroad all right. Only I was tired out as I was wet to my chin by crossing Bull Run Creek. Our General was wounded and has since died. I think we lost 2 thirds of the Brigade. Most of them were taken prisoners. Our company are all missing but 13. We know that 3 of them are killed and 4 of the 13 we have are wounded so the brigade was pretty well used up and discouraged.*

Our old Division Commander General Slocum came to us when we got to Alexandria and made a speech to us complimenting us for fighting Jackson Corps. So it appears we attacked Jackson's whole corps instead of a lot of guerillas as we at first supposed. When we got back to Alexandria our old Colonel Torbert was there to take command of the brigade. He has been absent since we were at Harrisons Landing. Knapsacks and rations were issued to us immediately and we were ordered to Bull Run again where we could hear them fighting very plain. We got to Chantilly in the evening and formed a line of battle behind the first line but we were not actively engaged here although we lost some men.

The next day after we got here, General Kearney's body was brought past us. He had been killed the day before. When they killed him, I think they killed the bravest and most dashing General in the Army.

We are now lying near our old camp Seminary but I expect to move soon. I will write if any thing new turns up.

Give my love to all,
from your afectionate son,
John P. Hamilton

1. Libby Prison was a Confederate prison in Richmond, Virginia, known for its high death toll. It was overcrowded and lacked sanitation, and its Union prisoners lived in squalor and starvation.
2. General Philip Kearny was shot on September 1, 1862, when he accidently rode into the Confederate lines during the action at Chantilly, Virginia.

Camp near Sharpsburg, Maryland
Oct the 12th, 1862

Dear Mother:

I received your letter and was glad to hear from you. Since I wrote you last we have been after the Rebs, but did not find them. We heard they were at Williamsport and we left camp in the night and marched 14 miles to Williamsport, but when we got there we found they had skedaddled. We stayed there a couple of days and then we came back here. We are now near the battle field of Antietam.

I have not seen Aleck in some time, but guess he is all right. For you know he belongs to McClellans Provost Guard and they dont have to go in a fight.

I have not heard from James but I think his regiment is still around Washington. The 15th New Jersey Regiment are out here now and have been assigned to our brigade. Our company have no officers now and we have only 13 privates in the company and our brigade General wants to break our company up for it is such a small company that we dont hardly make a show at all. He gives us the privilege of going in any company in the regiment or going into the 1st New Jersey Battery. I think I will try the Battery so dont be surprised if you hear in my next that I am in the Battery. The 23rd and 26th NJ Regiments are also here and belong to our brigade.

We all had a drill yesterday and one of the new regiments are as large as the whole of our old brigade.

Direct your letters as before and I will get them.

Love to all, from your son,
John P. Hamilton

Camp in Virginia[1]
Nov. the 8th, 1862

Dear Mother,

When I wrote you last I told you I thought I would join the battery and I am now in it and like it very well. I have been in it nearly a month now. We don't have to carry our knapsacks. They are carried on the Leimber boxes[2] *and we have no musket to carry so we can march very easy.*

Since I wrote you last we have been to Hagerstown and stayed a week and came back again to our old camp and the other night we got orders to march and started the next morning and now here we are in Virginia and bound for some place I dont know where. We had a pretty hard snow storm here yesterday and last night and it is commencing to feel like winter so I wish you would send me a pair of gloves by mail.

That piece of poetry you sent me about the two brothers at South Mountain, one in gray and the other in blue, I saw them myself. One of them belonged to Cobbs Legion of the Rebel Army and other belonged to our division. I think to the 16th New York. They were both wounded and died side by side. That picture of the battlefield that you sent me does very well. Only the artist has gone too far when he put the women on it for I aint saw any women on the battle field. Yet during a battle they generally wait until the battle is over or else they are in the rear but never so near the danger as the artist has put them on that picture. Although I suppose they would be on the field if they were let, but no soldier would let a woman come into such a dangerous place.

The Captain of the battery has wanted me to take a pair of horses but I think I would rather by a cannoneer for it is so much trouble to take care of horses in cold weather.

Give my love to all. I will write you again at the first opportunity.

From your afectionate son.
John P. Hamilton
Direct
John P. Hamilton
Battery A. lst N.J. Artillery
1st Division, 6th Corps

1. On November 7, President Lincoln relieved General McClellan of command of the Army of the Potomac and appointed General Ambrose Burnside to replace him.
2. Cannons were attached to two-wheeled carts called limbers. The limber also carried ammunition, stored in a limber box that sat atop the axel.

Camp of Battery A in position in front of Fredericksburg, Virginia
Dec. 17th, 1862

Dear Mother,

I write you a few lines to let you know that I am well and hope this finds you all the same. I suppose you must feel anxious to hear from me as you have not heard from me in so long a time. I have not wrote to you in some time because we were moving from one place to another and I could not find time and sometimes when I had time I had no paper or envelopes and where we are just now, we cannot buy any. The last sheet of paper you sent me I wrote a letter to Aleck with and the men in the Battery are not very obliging about lending paper. I got this sheet off one of the men by writing him a letter as he could not write himself.

For the last 5 days we have been in this position.[1] *The first two days the Rebs tried to drive us out but it was a long range fight and we have rifle guns and I guess we gave them the worst of it. Yesterday our section was sent down on the left to silence 4 of the rebel guns that was annoying the Infantry. They had their guns inside of good earth works and we had to go into position in the open field. We were in full view of them and we had only 2 guns and they made the gravel fly around for a while but as soon as we got unlimbered, we commenced at them and we had not fired over 10 shots before their fire slacked.*

They had the advantage of us because the wind blew toward us and every time they fired the smoke was between them and us and by the time the smoke cleared away they would be loaded again. But every time we fired the smoke would blow right behind us and we would have to stand up in open sight and load, but for all that we had not been in front of them ¾ of an hour before they limbered up and skedaddled out of their works. They had to run along the edge of the woods about half a mile before they got out of our sight and we kept the shell cracking around them as long as we could see them go. We lost 3 horses but none of our men got hit, but the infantry that laid behind us got the worst of it as nearly all of the Reb shells bust behind us.

I saw Jim and was with him one night. His regiment has been engaged but I do not know where his regiment is now and I don't know whether he was hurt or not, but I don't suppose he was or else I would have heard it for bad news always travels fast.

I received the gloves that you sent me all right and they came in good time for it is getting cold. I picked up another woolen blanket on the field and it comes very good for the nights are cold. We have not got paid in some time and it dont look now as if we would be in some time longer not until we get settled in some camp anyway and I dont know when that will be.

Give my best wishes to all enquiring friends and my love to Susie and Alice and mother and believe me your

Lucky son,
John

1. On December 13, the Union Army of the Potomac, commanded by Major General Ambrose E. Burnside, attacked Confederate positions held by the Army of Northern Virginia at Fredericksburg, Virginia. The Union attack was a complete failure.

Camp at White Oak Church, Virginia[1]
Jan. 7th, 1863

Dear Sister Mary,

I received your letter just now and having plenty of time, I will answer it. We are in a fine camp and we have built a log house. We have a large piece of canvas for the roof and it is very comfortable. We have a fireplace in it but we do not require any fire yet for it is quite warm yet, but the nights are cool.

The time passes very slow in camp. I wish you would send me something to read. Dear Sister, you dont know what a big thing you ask when you ask me to get a furlough. I might as well try to fly as to try to get a furlough. If I thought I could get one, I would try awful hard, but I see other men trying all kinds of ways to get one and cant, so I make myself as contented as I can although I would like to see you all again. But you must not worry about me for I am in good health and am very comfortable.

I went the other day to see George Fouratt. I hardly knew him he has so much whiskers. He is in good health but he has got enough of the Army already.

I have seen Brother Jim again. He is all right only he has got it into his head to try and go home when he gets paid. Furlough or no furlough it will take a smart man to go home without the proper papers and I told him if he tried it he would be shure to be caught and it might go hard with him. I told him he had better make up his mind to stay until his time was out and then he would be home as soon as I would.

Tell Mother to not think of sending me a box or present for I would never get it. I will send word when it will be safe to send one.

Give my regards to James, my love to all the children. Tell Mother I got the 75 cents.

From your afectionate brother,
John P. Hamilton

1. Approximately five miles east of Fredericksburg.

Chapter 10

Ague, Fever and Brandreth's Special Pills

The only thing he gives is quinine...no matter what is the matter with you...I had a pretty tough time with my throat...I have been on a hospital boat.
–February 1863, camp near White Oak Church, Virginia

Medicine at the start of the Civil War was rudimentary at best. The causes of infection were not well understood, although a few crusader organizations, like the New York Sanitary Commission, advocated proper sanitation to stem the widespread growth of disease. Meanwhile in Europe, French chemist and microbiologist Louis Pasteur was conducting experiments to prove germ theory and encouraged doctors to sanitize their hands and instruments prior to surgery. In reality, few doctors practiced either protocol.

Disease ran rampant in the camps. The crowded conditions, poor hygiene, dampness and inadequate shelter, along with poor clothing and deficient diet, contributed to widespread illness. Twice as many men succumbed to disease than to gun wounds in the war, although amputations were a more dramatic vestige of the conflict.

Once army basic supplies and clothing were issued, soldiers had to scramble to replace or add to their supplies to keep the elements at bay. John lost his shoes running through muck during a skirmish, a common occurrence, and when he found a pair on a dead man, had no time to put them on. Shoes and coats were premium items and kept the men protected against the cold and damp weather.

In early September 1861, John wrote home that his best friend Jim Furlong suffered "from a fever and ague very bad." Ague, a fever with successive stages of a high temperature and chills, was a common ailment in mid-nineteenth-century America. The term "ague" was often associated with the flu, but it also described shaking chills accompanied by pains in the bones and joints. A far worse illness was malaria, which also presented with fever and joint pain, accompanied by vomiting, anemia and jaundice. If left untreated, convulsions and death followed.

Jim was not the only one to become sick. He wrote to his mother, "I had a slight touch of them [fever and ague], but it did not get a hold of me hard enough and I shook it off in two days." The universal remedy for ague, intermittent fevers, colds and malaria was the "wonder drug" of its day, quinine. Known for its ability to stop the symptoms of malaria, quinine is extracted from the bark of the cinchona tree in South America.

The Union army was well acquainted with the benefits of quinine, purchasing more than 500,000 five-ounce tins of quinine sulphate during the war. It proved to be an auspicious purchase. It was estimated that one out of every four cases of disease during the war was malaria, and the best treatment was, indeed, quinine.

The swamps of the South, damp climate, rain and cold that the soldiers endured exacerbated the numbers of those stricken. Men marched shoulder to shoulder and slept side by side in close quarters. Camps were breeding grounds not only for malaria but also mumps, measles and chickenpox. John's brother James's regiment suffered an outbreak of measles that incapacitated the regiment and kept many quarantined.

For more serious epidemics like malaria, it is estimated that more than 1 million Union soldiers contracted the illness during the war, and outbreaks were common. In May 1862, John wrote to his mother, "The climate is very unhealthy here for the days are very hot and the nights are cold and damp and to guard against fevers and ague we get a gill of whiskey mixed with quinine."

The quinine treatment worked primarily to reduce body temperature, while the four ounces of whiskey acted as a chaser and cut the bitterness of the quinine. It worked. As John related, "I have good health and have not seen a days sickness since I have been in the Army," except for the two days at the start of the war when he and Jim were sick.

John also reminded his mother that if he needed medicine in camp, he must report to the orderly sergeant, who will take him to a doctor, and "the only thing he gives you is quinine…no matter what is the matter with you." Quinine, it seems, was the universal treatment for what ailed the soldiers.

When John was growing up, there were common beliefs concerning the promotion of good health. Drinking porter or stout—a dark, heavy beer—was one. John recommended his mother drink porter when she felt unwell. It was thought that the heavy malts in porter or stout increased general good health. Toward the end of the war, John advised his mother to use the money he sent home. He told her, "If you don't do anything else, buy good things to eat and buy the best porter for yourself to drink."

The popularity of Brandreth's Pills was due to the advertising genius of its founder. Brandreth's Allock Manufacturing Company produced both porous plasters and pills. *Virginia S. Brandreth.*

He recalled for his mother the time he worked for Samuel R. March, a New Brunswick baker located on Neilson Street. Mrs. March, John wrote, used to send him daily to the drugstore for "a bottle of brown stout porter. I suppose that is what made her so healthy." It is thought that Mrs. March was a solidly built woman, no doubt a result of her daily intake of stout, which easily added pounds.

The other product John found useful at the New Brunswick drugstore was Dr. Brandreth's Pills, a universal household remedy in the United States thanks to the marketing genius of its creator. The pills, an invention of Benjamin Brandreth's grandfather, were alleged to cure many diseases by purging toxins out of the blood. The formula for the original "Vegetable Universal Pill" was a strong cathartic based on the belief that impurity of the blood was the cause of many illnesses.

An extremely successful businessman without a medical diploma, Benjamin Brandreth and his potent medicine were well known. Brandreth was a pioneer in mass advertising, taking ads and placing testimonials in books, pamphlets and newspapers. The Brandreth Pill Works was established in Ossining, New York, in 1838 and became a multimillion-dollar business, an astronomical amount of money for the time, worth more than $28 million in today's dollars.

John asked his mother to send him a box of Brandreth's Pills. When he received them, he wrote home, "I used some of the pills and gave the rest of them to some of the Boys." Later, toward the end of John's enlistment, he broke out in pimples. "I wish you would send me a box of Brandreth's Pills or anything you think will be good to clear out my blood."

Like the tonics of the day, Brandreth's magic pills were thought to cure a range of ailments. Brandreth, who emigrated from England to America in 1835, brought with him his family and his grandfather's formula for the "magic" pills. The Universal Vegetable Pills contained sarsaparilla, aloes, gamboges and cobeynth—some of the most powerful cathartics in the botanical field.

Overindulgence in fatty foods, city living with little or no exercise and poor digestion contributed to the growth of industries offering purgatives and purges of various potency in the mid-nineteenth century. Physicians, such as they were, regularly prescribed purges; it was the most popular remedy of its day for poor digestion. It also generated another industry: quacks and other dubious purveyors of patent medicines, who pursued the sick with this popular diagnosis of "indigestion" and offered their own specially patented concoctions containing often frightening substances.

In many cases, the ingredients of these medicines were unknown or contained narcotics, alcohol or actual poisons like mercury. These "quack" medicines were, if not outright deadly, at least addictive since there was no regulation of their ingredients. Newspaper and magazine advertising often exaggerated the claims of their remedies.

Brandreth's Pills, however, was one of the most popular patent medicines. Brandreth often scorned his competitors and argued that his pills were vegetable based and had been used without one "fatal consequence": "A dose more of Brandreth's Pills than required will never hurt you, but not taking a dose when required, may cost you your life."

One of Brandreth's advertising pamphlets exhorted his customers to "Purge then, ye wise, before your sickness is too far advanced, and by the blessing of God, and Brandreth's Pills, insure your safety and your life."

Jan. 16th 1863

Dear Mother,

I write you a few lines to let you know how I am getting along. I cant say I am well for I have a bad cold and a very sore throat but I am in a good place. I am in the Battery Hospital. We have a sheet iron stove and a comfortable bed to sleep in.

I saw in yesterday's Herald that Addams Express will send packages and boxes to Burnsides Army, so if you think proper, you can send me a box.

We have not been paid yet and dont know when we will. We can only get tobacco once in a while and then we have to pay a big price for it.

I have not heard from Aleck in a long time. The last I heard from him he was at Alexandria.

Give my love to Mary Jane and all the children, to Susie and Alice.

Your afectionate son,
John
Direct John P. Hamilton, 1st N.J. Vol. Artillery, Battery A, 1st Division, 6 corps
Washington, D.C.

Camp near White Oak Church, Virginia
Feb. 1863

Dear Mother,

To let you know I am well again. I had a pretty tough time with my throat but as soon as it commenced to get better I was not long in getting all right.

Since I wrote you before I have been on a hospital boat and while I was on it, we went to Alexandria for coal. I could have easy have deserted if I had wanted to. I am with the Battery again now. I got back just in time to get my pay. We got 78 dollars. I owed a little money in the Battery.

I will send you 60 dollars as soon as I can get a receipt from the 1st Regiment. They have not been paid yet so you look out for it. This money I send home, I want you to use.

Tell Father to write to Jim for he has got a notion he wants to come home and, of course, he cannot without getting in trouble and if Father writes him a good letter, it may do him good.

Give my love to all.

Your afectionate son,
John

Chapter 11

The Ladies Aid Societies and "Dragon" Dix

[Y]*esterday I got the box. It had been broken open and the jar of preserves taken out.*
–March 18, 1863, White Oak Church, Virginia

New Brunswick, in addition to its many churches and missions, boasted numerous charitable organizations to which its residents could express their generosity. The Humane Society, established in 1807, supplied the city's poor with coal in winter, while the women of the Dorcas Society helped to clothe destitute widows and their children beginning with its establishment in 1813. There also was the Ladies Depository, which supplied work to "respectable families," and the New Brunswick Orphans Asylum, an auxiliary to the Newark Orphans Asylum, created in 1860.

The start of the war, however, raised the level of commitment for patriotism and care. Both in the North and South, the first efforts of support for soldiers came from their families, especially the wives and mothers who, like John's mother, arranged care packages of jams and cheese to fortify their boys, occasionally including a bottle of wine.

Many soldiers, however, came from poorer families or did not have families and relied on the compassion of others. John often shared his food packages from home with his best friend Jim Furlong and others in his regiment who might not have been so fortunate. Relief societies and soldier aid societies were started to support the men at war, and eventually, there was even an official government agency for these groups.

The United States Sanitary Commission was created by federal legislation in 1861 to oversee and coordinate the volunteer efforts of women who wanted to contribute to the war effort of the Union states. These women were the wives, sisters, mothers, children and sweethearts of soldiers, as well as neighbors and friends. In many instances, those at home had watched their sole financial and emotional support march away to unfamiliar surroundings and to grave physical danger from the diseases of camp life and the gunfire of the battlefield.

Other organizations—including the Ladies Hospital Aid Society, the Union Volunteer Refreshment Saloon and the United States Christian Commission—were started in Northern cities to bring additional comfort to soldiers fighting the war. Members performed a variety of jobs, including sewing shirts and quilts, collecting medical supplies, knitting socks, gathering foodstuffs for care packages and writing letters, as well as holding social functions such as picnics, pageants and fairs to raise money for the Sanitary Commission.

A staggering twenty thousand soldiers' relief societies sprung up throughout the North and South within two weeks of the attack on Fort Sumter, but in the North, the support from the U.S. Sanitary Commission ensured that these relief efforts were effective by coordinating needed supplies and arranging transport. Everyone in New Brunswick either had a direct relative in the war or was close friends with one. It is certain that the city women, either through their churches or informally in their homes, contributed to the war effort by collecting foodstuffs, knitting, raising cash donations and performing other good works. Although there is no direct corroboration that Mary Ann Hamilton belonged to such a group, her single-handed efforts in sending packages to her son obviously benefited not only John but his fellow soldiers.

John's sister, Mary Jane, newly married with a baby and living in Newark with her husband, James Fouratt, most likely joined that city's relief organization in April 1861. Newark was one of the first cities in the state to form a Soldiers' Relief Society, and Mary Jane would have participated on behalf of brother John and father Alexander, as well as her other brothers Aleck and soon-to-be enlisted James, all soldiers for the Union.

Women volunteers also extended their aid efforts by tending to the wounded. The two military hospitals in New Jersey, the Centre Street Military Hospital in Newark, Essex County, and the Beverly Army Hospital in Beverly, Burlington County, together accommodated about two thousand men. It is a historical fact that women volunteers brought food, oversaw catering, made or repaired clothing and managed the housekeeping of the military hospitals.

Perhaps John's sister was a participant in the May 31, 1862 Ladies Aid Meeting in Newark, as reported by the *Newark Daily Advertiser* on May 30, 1862: "[It met to] make the usual arrangements for the ensuing week. It is believed the women of Newark feel a deep interest in everything connected with this hospital, and the care of our sick and wounded soldiers, and only desire to know how they can be really useful."

Another prominent role for women was nursing, a field traditionally reserved for men. Prior to the war, women were not trained to nurse and were considered to be a nuisance in a medical setting. It was feared that women would "lose their morality" by nursing soldiers, but the necessity of medical care and lack of men to do the job left the work to a cadre of women volunteers.

The Army Nursing Services was established shortly after the Civil War began; sixty-year-old Dorothea Dix, social reformer and teacher, was named as superintendent of women nurses. Miss Dix quickly established rigid qualifications for her volunteer nurses, who were mostly middle-class women, relatives or friends of those serving. Each candidate, Miss Dix wrote, must be "past 30 years of age, healthy, plain almost to repulsion in dress and devoid of personal attractions." They must also be able to "cook all kinds of low diet" and avoid "colored dresses, hoops, curls, jewelry and flowers on their bonnets." They also could not associate with surgeons or patients socially and were to be considered the "senior attendants" in the wards.

Miss Dix, seemingly a caring, compassionate individual by most accounts, was feared by her nurses, who referred to her as "Dragon" Dix behind her back. It can be surmised that many fathers did not want their daughters in a medical environment either, as male nurses still outnumbered female nurses four to one during the war. Regardless of Miss Dix's constraints or those of society, thousands of women applied for nursing positions. Their contributions to the health and care of the wounded cannot be overemphasized.

Women nurses had three distinct functions, according to historian Daniel J. Hoisington. They regulated, prepared and served patients their meals in the hospital; managed the physical needs of patients distributing linens and clothing; and, finally, cared for the emotional and spiritual needs of the soldiers.

Dorothea Dix, social reformer and teacher, directed the women's nursing program in the Civil War. Some of the women are pictured here with U.S. Sanitary Commission officers. *Library of Congress.*

Women who occupied the food management positions were called "superintendents of special diet" and were responsible for ensuring that the patient received the diet the doctor prescribed for him. Surgeons prescribed a patient a "full," "half" or "low" diet. A low diet, for instance, was for the seriously ill and consisted of coffee and toast or farina. It was the nurses' responsibility to make sure each patient ate the prescribed diet.

Those nurses assigned to the physical needs of patients obtained clothing, linens and supplies, which they received from the various aid societies associated with the U.S. Sanitary Commission. Other nurses acted as surrogate family members, providing comfort to soldiers by writing letters, reading, sitting with them or singing songs. For the wounded, these angels of mercy took on the roles of absent wife, mother, sister or daughter. Women nurses, however, rarely assisted in surgeries with patients.

There is good reason to believe that John came into direct contact with female nurses during his stay on the hospital ship in 1863. While John does not identify by name the hospital ship he was on, in January 1863, he suffered from "a bad cold and a very sore throat" and was placed first in a battery hospital, which was a field hospital either in the open air or tent, holding about six patients. Later, as the seriousness of his condition progressed, he was moved to a hospital ship. Transporting the wounded from field hospitals to floating hospitals and then to general hospitals in major hubs, like Alexandria, Virginia, was common at the start of the war.

He wrote to his mother in mid-January 1863, "I am in the Battery Hospital. We have a sheet iron stove and a comfortable bed to sleep in." Later, in February, he wrote, "I had a pretty tough time with my throat but as soon as it commenced to get better I was not long in getting all right…I have been on a hospital boat."

He was fortunate to be transferred to a hospital ship. Fleet surgeon Ninian A. Pickney recounted that "there is less…sickness in the Fleet than in the healthiest portion of the globe." Although John did not name the ship, if it was similar to ships like the *Daniel Webster No. 2* or the *Kennebeck*, then John may have been cared for by women in the Catholic order of the Sisters of the Holy Cross or Sisters of Charity or even by a few lay women acting as nurses' aides. These women were the forerunners of the U.S. Navy Nurse Corps. The good care John received on the ship no doubt spurred his full recovery to health.

The ladies aid societies, whether organized as informal sewing circles or formally organized groups, were the backbone of the civilian volunteer war effort. As noted earlier, they helped to fund the United States Sanitary Commission through their money-raising efforts, the most notable being the June 1864 Central Fair, a "fair extraordinaire" in Philadelphia. Organized by the women of Pennsylvania, New Jersey and Delaware, the fair raised $1 million for the war effort, a significant contribution even today and an enormous amount of money for the time.

Despite their added duties as acting heads of households in the absence of husbands and sons and, in some cases, as the guardians of family

The hospital ship *Nashville* was similar to the type of floating hospital where John recuperated from his "bad throat." *Library of Congress.*

businesses, women generously volunteered, giving time and effort to aid their soldier boys. Along with the many changes the Civil War brought, this one is revolutionary: it was the first time that women left the home hearth to take an active role in the outside world. It did, in fact, open a world of possibilities for women when the war ended. Although there was no feminist movement in the modern sense, historian Mary Elizabeth Massey commented in her 1966 book *Bonnet Brigades: American Women and the Civil War*, "It was going to be impossible to keep the 'girls' quiet and docile after four noisy, active years."

White Oak Church, Virginia
April 2nd, 1863

Dear Mother,

I write you a few lines to let you know I received your letter day before yesterday and was glad to hear from you and that you had received my picture safe. You say you think I am growing slim. You must remember I have grown tall since you saw me last. I am now 5 feet 9 ½ inches high and weigh 150 pounds so I am not so slim as I look in the picture.

I suppose you are thinking of Aleck today for it is his birthday. I have had a letter from him and have answered it. He was in Murfreesboro, Tenn.

I saw Jim the other day. He looks well. The boots you sent him fit him, but I think you paid too much for them. I could get a better pair out here now for the money. I can tell you all that was in the box when I get it and then you will know what was stolen: one jar of butter, one cake, two loaves bread, a paper full of crackers, hickory nuts, little cakes and crackers, one paper of pepper, one of sugar, one of dried peaches and three or four weekly papers. There were no books or handkerchief or preserves.

The butter lasted me until last night and it was fine. I have not got any money to buy tobacco. I don't know when we will be paid.

Ben Moffit is coming home on furlough. He has got a commission as lieutenant. I am agoing to send my watch home by him to get fixed. I wish I could get a commission as lieutenant. I suppose I could if I had some friend who had influence and then I could get a furlough and come home and see you.

The roads are getting dry and good and if they stay so long, I think we will be on the move.

Give my love to Mary Jane and Jim and tell them not to think hard of me for not writing to them for I do not always have the time and paper and, of course, I write to you and they hear from me.

My love to all.

Your afectionate son,
John

Camp of Battery A in Virginia.
May 7th, 1863

Dear Mother,

You will see by the heading of this letter that we have moved. We crossed the river in front of Fredericksburg and on the morning of the 3rd we took the city and advanced over the heights to a place called Mays Farm.[1] *Before we met the Rebs again, they made a stand and charged our battery three times. The last time they charged was they came very close to us but every man stood by the guns and we were giving them double rounds of canister. The battery right along side of us the men ran away from their guns. It was a Maryland Battery. It was a hard afternoons work.*

We worked in our shirt sleeves at the guns steady from about 3 o'clock until after dark and our guns were so hot that the black paint on them was all blisters. That night we crossed back over the river at United States ford. Our battery had the position of honor that night. We went into position to cover the ford and were the last battery that crossed. We lost 2 horses killed and two men wounded in our battery. We all had some very narrow escapes but it is not worth while to tell you them now. I will wait until I get home and then they will be nice to talk about if my life is spared to see it.

There has been an order that we could not send any letters home and I dont know as you will get this. I have not heard anything of Jim. I expect he was engaged up on the right near Chancellorsville. We have orders to move tomorrow morning. I dont know where.

Love to all.

Your afectionate son,
John

1. Beginning on April 27, Major General Hooker maneuvered the Union Army of the Potomac to attack the Confederate Army of Northern Virginia. A major battle was fought at Chancellorsville, several miles west of Fredericksburg, on May 1 and 2, as well as a secondary battle at Fredericksburg and Salem Church on May 3 and 4. The Union army was again defeated.

Camp near White Oak Church, Virginia
May 15th, 1863

Dear Mother,

We are in our old camp again. I heard some bad rumors about James so I got a horse and went over to his old camp. I found 2 or 3 of this company in camp. The regiment were on picket.

The men that I saw of his company were regular shirks and I did not put much confidence in what they said. They told me that James was killed on the 3rd at Chancellorsville but they were not there and it may not be so. He may have been taken prisoner. I shall not believe it until I have to for I remember at the Battle of Gaines Hills, 2 men of Captain Fouratts' company were supposed to have been killed and were marked dark on the company books and they both turned up again. One of them was Peter McGovern and the other was called Jackalow.

I will hunt the news up all I can and let you know as soon as I find out anything.

Love to all.

Your afectionate, son,
John

Camp near White Oak Church, Virginia
May 29, 1863

Dear Mother,

I write you to let you know I am well and received your letter yesterday. I was not surprised to hear of James' death. I had made up my mind that it was so. I am a going over to this regiment tomorrow and see if he left anything that I can send home for a keepsake and if I find anything I will take it over the 28th N.J. and give them to Sailor Bill to take home as their time is about up.

If you get this letter before Ben Moffit leaves Brunswick, I wish you would send me two woolen shirts, some kind of gray stuff. Dont send knit shirts for they are bad about getting the lice out of them when they get into them.

I have got plenty of paper and stamps to last me 4 or 5 months.

Mother, you must see a lawyer and see if you cannot get James' 100 dollars bounty. I have heard you can get it.

Give my love to all.

From your afectionate son,
John

On the Banks of the Rappahannock, Virginia
June 8th, 1863[1]

Dear Mother,

I write you a few lines to let you know how I am getting along. I received the shirts and was glad to get them. I was offered $4.00 for one of them but I will keep them for they are just the things I want.

We have not been engaged yet. Two or three batterys have crossed over and are in position behinds works.

Since I wrote you last I went to see the orderly sergeant of James' company and he told me all the particulars about James' death. He says he was hit with a shell or solid shot. It cut one of his legs off and the calf of his other leg and he died while the doctors were at work on him.

There was a dress coat in the company that belonged to him so I took it and gave it to Sailor Bill to bring home to you. I also send you by him a Derringer pistol which Father gave me. He found it on the field at Fair Oaks.

I have not heard from Aleck in some time. I wrote to him of James' death but I suppose their army is moving and he has not got my letter.

I dont believe we will do much fighting here this time for we are not advancing the same as we did before. We are strengthening our position on the other side of the river every night and we are putting a 100 pound Parrot gun in position on this side of the River opposite Fredericksburg.

Enclosed you will find 15 dollars.

Give my love to all.

Your afectionate son,
John

1. General Lee had already begun moving portions of the Confederate army away from the Fredericksburg area toward the Shenandoah Valley to position the army for another invasion of the North.

Chapter 12

Sisters on the Homefront

I will write Susan and Alice a letter as soon as I get time.
–April 21, 1863, White Oak Church, Virginia

The three Hamilton girls—Mary Jane, who in 1861 was twenty-two; Susan, twelve; and Alice, nine—enlivened the Hamilton home with laughter, friends and playful antics. Panto, the younger girls' pet dog, added comic relief to a household devoid of men and to the process of waiting from letter to letter to learn how their menfolk fared.

Mary Jane, single and living with her parents, the norm for the time, worked as a weaver in the cotton factory. There, she met James W. Fouratt of North Brunswick, an adjacent township, who became her husband on January 1, 1861, a few months before the start of the war. It was a simple wedding as befitting the Hamiltons' social status, with both her parents, Alexander and Mary Ann, witnessing the ceremony.

Mary Jane left her job in the factory when she married. Her new full-time work, like most married women in the mid-nineteenth century who could afford it, would center on keeping house for her husband and the eventual, hoped-for family. Fouratt, a cutter who worked with milling machines, moved with Mary Jane to Newark, where his family lived, shortly after the wedding. Before the close of the year, Mary Jane and James would be the proud parents of a daughter, Mary Ida.

As soon as a girl was "old enough," it was not unusual for families to put her out to work in a factory or store until she was married. Even though girls

Often, the fate of the poor was to send their children to work. Here two young girls, ages twelve and eleven, work as millworkers. *Library of Congress.*

and women earned less than boys and men, the added income for working-class families was necessary to make ends meet. When John joined the war in June 1861, followed by father Alexander and then brother James, the household was left without any regular income stream. John sent his mother all or part of his pay throughout the war, and we can infer that Alexander and James did the same. Yet it must have been a financial struggle for those remaining at home.

Susie, although old enough to work at twelve years old, was not sent to the factory. Up until she was ten, Susie was sickly, suffering from what her mother described as "epileptic" fits. A neurological disorder, epilepsy is often defined by convulsions and fits. It is impossible to diagnose Susie a century and a half later from the limited information provided, but her later hospitalizations lend credence to her suffering from a physical disability that also caused her great mental anguish and depression.

Both Susie and her nine-year-old sister, Alice, were home-schooled by their mother, learning to read and write. At the time, only a handful of states provided universal free public education to children, but New Jersey was not one of them. Local church organizations or charities were available to provide schooling if parents declared themselves paupers, although most were not willing to subject themselves to such stigma.

A payment system, called a "rate bill," was used for partial financial support of schools. The rate bill was a tuition fee based on the number of children in a family attending school. Sadly, many of the working poor could not afford to pay it. Although many states modified aid for public schools in the 1860s, New Jersey was the last state to abolish the rate bill, making schools free in 1871.

John complimented the girls on their home-schooling, especially their writing skills. About nine-year-old Alice in early 1862, he wrote that she "must be a smart girl to write her name so well." He requested that she "sign her name to the next letter" as practice. It also helped to assuage the loneliness and homesickness that he often must have felt as he recalled the many nights at the kitchen table when he watched the girls practice their lessons. He remembered it well. "I almost think I can see her writing just as she use to on the slate."

Not to be forgotten, sister Susie, twelve, was critiqued on her writing ability, too. "Tell Susie I think she is improving in her writing," he wrote encouragingly. It may have been because of her medical condition, but from the tone and attention given to her in his letters, John seemed to favor Susie.

John sympathized with Susie's unhappiness and laughed with her predicaments. When Susie's pet quail birds died in 1863, John expressed his condolences, but when she complained that the family dog, Panto, had fleas, he joked to his mother, "Tell her to put him in a pot and boil him and that will take all the fleas away."

Susie wrote John a rare letter just before Christmas 1863 that must have lifted her brother's spirits immensely. In response, John wrote back to her and recalled past holidays with the family and Jim Furlong and ended by enclosing five dollars, a generous amount of money for Susie to buy presents for herself and Alice.

John was placed in a peculiar role in late 1863. Their father had been seriously wounded and was near death; their oldest brother, Aleck, was a shadowy memory; and their youngest brother, James, had been killed in battle. As their closest remaining brother, John was the logical choice for the role of surrogate father to his sisters. He certainly felt responsible that the girls have a pleasant holiday. In writing to Susie, he directed her to "buy something nice and it will be the same as if I were there...that is if you can think so."

Married sister Mary Jane, residing in Newark, sent John letters and gift boxes, which he appreciated, and Alice tried to impress him with her efforts at handwriting, but it was Susie who charmed him. Just after their father died in January 1864, John sent Susie a small locket with his photograph in it. Perhaps he expected that it would comfort her after their father's death. It came with some sacrifice. John sold his watch to pay for the photograph.

He complimented both girls when he heard from two of his fellow soldiers who visited Mrs. Hamilton and Furlong's father while on furlough in New Brunswick: "They told me that Susan is a large girl nearly as tall as men and Alice is also a fine girl."

Later, John told his mother that one of the Brunswick Boys, John Vroom, also promised to visit Mrs. Hamilton on his furlough. He asked his mother to provide a photograph of Susie, Alice and herself as a keepsake that Vroom could bring to him in camp. He loved and missed his family, and a photograph would be a constant reminder for him of his waiting family.

Camp near Taneytown, Maryland
July 1st, 1863[1]

Dear Mother,

I write you a few lines to let you know I am well. We have been in Maryland about a week now and are only three miles from Pennsylvania. We are still in the reserve artillery. The people around here are better than in Virginia. We can buy milk and other things at a reasonable price and often get things for nothing and almost every house we pass they have water and glasses sitting out at the door for the soldiers to drink and sometimes a pretty girl comes out and serves it to us.

I have not had a letter from anybody in a long time. I suppose Sailor Bill and Bill Furlong are home now and I guess Furlong is glad for I never saw anybody want to get home as bad as he did. I suppose Sailor Bill gave you the coat and pistol. I suppose by the time you get this, it will be 4th of July. I suppose we will be firing salutes by that time but if we are, I think we will fire it with shot and shell.

Give my love to all enquiring friends and write soon.

From your afectionate son.
John

1. Although John appeared unaware of it, the three-day Battle of Gettysburg had begun on this date about fifteen miles north of Taneytown in Pennsylvania.

Camp near Boonsboro, Maryland
July 11th, 1863

Dear Mother,

I must write and let you know the news for I suppose you have heard of the Battle of Gettysburg and are anxious to hear from me. Well, I am all right but it was a hot place especially for Artillery. It was the heaviest artillery fight of the war. We lost two men killed and six men wounded. One of the men killed was hit right alongside of me. He was an old man about 60 years old. Our gun carriage and wheels were pretty well marked with musket balls. We worked the guns in our shirt sleeves it was so hot. I did not get touched.

The battle[1] *was on the 3rd and on the 4th we stood by our guns all day and it rained hard nearly all day but there was no fighting, but it was the worst 4th of July I ever experienced for there were so many dead on the field and they smelt awful.*

I have had no letter from you. When you write let me know if you got a letter from me with 15 dollars in it. I have heard nothing from Aleck. Our captain is with us now.

Give my love to Susie and Alice.

Your afectionate son,
John

1. The Battle of Gettysburg began on July 1 and ended on July 3. The Confederate army, having exhausted itself attacking the Union positions, began retreating back to Virginia on July 4.

Camp near Rappahannock Station, Virginia
August 18, 1863

Dear Mother,

I received Susan's letter this morning and was glad to hear from you all. We are in the same camp as when I wrote you last. Our soft bread has stopped and we are on hard tack again. Our sutler came last night so we can get plenty of tobacco and knickknacks.

We are in a bad camp on account of water. We have to go about half a mile to get water. We have been digging a well. We got it down about 12 feet and it rained last night and this morning the well was full of muddy water but we are agoing to clean it out and try again.

While I write, I hear heavy firing over the river but I guess it is nothing but cavalry and the light artillery.

Tell Susie I am sorry her quails are dead and also that Panto has got fleas. Tell her to put him in a pot and boil him and that will take all the fleas away.

I wrote you a letter day before yesterday and enclosed 15 dollars.

Give my love to all.

Your afectionate son,
John P. Hamilton

Camp near Rappahannock, Virginia
Sept. 1st, 1863

Dear Mother,

I am well and hope you are all the same. I got a letter from you last night also the postage stamps, handkerchief and pills. I used some of the pills and gave the rest of them to some of the Boys.

I have had a letter from Aleck. He was telling me about the last battle he was in and about his marching without anything to eat. I know by experience that he must have hard times but I think we will be home by this time next year where we will have better times.

I was surprised to hear that Mat Severance was home and surprised also to hear that he says he was pressed into the Southern army. I guess he forgets the last letter he wrote to me from Savannah before the War (you will find it in my trunk) where he told me he thought the South were right and intended to fight for them and in the same letter he says I am enlisted and am a going to Fort Pulaski tomorrow morning.

If he thought they were right, he ought to have stuck to them and not deserted them when they needed men so bad but I guess the racket we gave them at Gettysburg made him sick of the business. Tell him if you see him again that I took a prisoner at Crampton's Pass who knew him. He told me that Aleck was sick when Fort Pulaski was taken and that he afterwards joined the Washington artillery.

Write soon. Love to all from your son,
John

Chapter 13

Mr. Meyer's Profitable Factories

I hope the Rubber Company was not mean enough to charge you anything for that pipe and if they did, let me know and I will send it back to them.
—February 23, 1864, camp near Brandy Station, Virginia

Christopher Meyer epitomized the rags-to-riches American dream. An enterprising German who immigrated to America at fifteen years old, Meyer owned the Meyer Rubber Company and its subsidiary businesses in New Brunswick, where the Hamilton men and their friends worked. Years later, Meyer's business would become one of the founding companies of United States Rubber Company, and Meyer would become a multimillionaire and philanthropist.

Working first in New York City as a machinist, Meyer moved to the central New Jersey area to install machinery for Horace Day, one of the first manufacturers of rubber goods. Under the auspices of the Goodyear rubber patent, Meyer improved the machinery, invented new machinery and perfected the manufacturer of rubber shoes, making them more durable and the shoemaking process less smelly.

Meyer and Day parted company, and in 1841, the former operated a small plant for two years at Landing Bridge on the Raritan Canal. The Meyer Rubber Company manufactured "shirred goods," decorative items gathered by drawing material along two or more parallel lines of stitching, as well as rubber shoes and carriage cloth. Unfortunately, a fire in 1845 destroyed the building and left Meyer penniless.

Christopher Meyer was a self-made millionaire who operated several industrial companies in New Brunswick. *From* History of Union and Middlesex Counties, New Jersey, with Illustrations, *edited by W. Woodford Clayton, 1882.*

Down but not out, Meyer engaged a new business partner, New York businessman John R. Ford, and the factory was rebuilt. The new firm of Ford and Company existed until 1850, when a joint stock company was formed under the name Ford Rubber Company with Meyer as president and Ford as treasurer. During the Mexican-American War (1846–48), the company also manufactured rubber pontoon bridges (temporary floating bridges used for river crossings) and boats for use by the United States government. Meyer went on to organize in 1849 the New Jersey Rubber Shoe Company, where the Hamilton men (Alexander, John and James) all eventually worked. The factory buildings were located in Washington Street near Peace Street.

In time, Meyer erected a larger factory on Little Burnet Street in New Brunswick where shoes, canes and boats were made. More than three hundred employees produced 500,000 pairs of rubber boots and shoes at the factory, amounting to nearly $700,000 in sales, worth about $18 million today.

In 1855, Meyer established the Novelty Rubber Works on Neilson Street, New Brunswick, for the manufacture of hard rubber products, including buttons, pipes, pipe stems and bowls, pipe and tobacco boxes, cigar cases, matchboxes and similar items. This is the same factory where John obtained his pipes during the war.

The goods manufactured at Novelty amounted to nearly $600,000 per year, and its products were shipped to all parts of the world. A "one-stop shopping" entity before the phrase was coined, Meyer dedicated the upper story of the main building for a paper-box manufacturing area that supplied the works with boxes for shipment of their goods.

Like many owners of Northern factories during the 1860s, Meyer recruited recently arrived immigrants and especially women and children, who worked for lower wages than men. Although skilled workmen like Alexander Hamilton and his son John made up a large percentage of the workers, such men were paid at a higher rate and were more costly to employ. An average male factory worker in 1860 earned about $20 per month, or $240 per year.

With the advent of the war, however, most of the young men who worked in the factory jumped at the chance to enlist in the Volunteers with the hopes of higher pay. A private in the Volunteers earned only about thirteen dollars per month, but with the prospect of a promotion, he could double or triple what the factory paid. Furthermore, most of the factory boys believed that the army was a less formidable task master than the bosses who oversaw them during the long days they toiled in the hot, often dangerous and confined surroundings of the factory.

According to the *Weeks Report* (a compilation included with the 1880 U.S. Census) and the *Aldrich Report* (the 1893 report of the U.S. Senate Committee on Finance), the estimated hourly workweek at United States factories in 1860 was between sixty-two and sixty-six hours, which included a half day on Saturdays. A "normal" eleven-hour workday was tedious and exceedingly long. The army at least promised adventure, travel, fresh air, exercise and plenty of outdoor living.

Next to textile manufacturing, shoemaking was the nation's leading industry. At the start of the war in 1861, these two industries initially suffered steep declines as the uncertain direction a war might take unnerved the commercial sector. Virtually overnight, the nation's businesses were in serious trouble. "Never before perhaps in the history of this country has such a feeling of uncertainty, of alternate hope and fear, prevailed in the business community," noted the *New York Tribune*. Thousands of businesses, large and small, failed that year as the loss of Southern markets combined with the loss

The New Jersey Rubber Company, owned by Christopher Meyer, produced all manner of rubber products during the Civil War. *From* History of Union and Middlesex Counties, New Jersey, with Illustrations, *edited by W. Woodford Clayton, 1882.*

of skilled workers to the army proved calamitous. However, as is often the case, the war would bring a change of fortune to these and other industries through army contracts and other war-generated business.

Historically, it is interesting to note that sometimes the right invention comes along at the right time. In this particular moment, it was the invention of a shoe-stitching machine that transformed the production of shoes from a handmade craft to a mass industry just before the war began. When the army needed to supply thousands of troops with shoes in a short time, Lyman Reed Blake's shoe-sewing machine invention allowed factories to double and then triple their production. The machines eliminated heavy, slow and tedious hand sewing and allowed the soles of the shoes to be attached to the uppers by machine stitching.

"A worker in a shoe factory could now turn out several hundred pairs a day," it was reported. Consequently, profits increased significantly, too. Meyer did not, like many other industries, have to retool or transform his factories to produce shoes or buttons for the army. He already had the capability for high production. The only resource in short supply was labor.

Many of the Brunswick Boys—like Martin Connelly, George Fouratt, Jim and William Furlong, John Tyler Lewis, Ben Moffett and Michael Welsh—worked with John in the factory. When they and their co-worker friends enlisted in the war, Meyer lost many of his skilled workers. While Irish and German immigrants moved to the city and provided cheap labor, it was women, especially those who were poor or whose husbands and sons left for war, who were enticed to work to support their families. The textile mills of Massachusetts were filled with women who carried the production, so why not the shoemaking industry?

By 1861, native and immigrant women composed 50 percent of all industrial workers; they filled the least-skilled and lowest-paying positions. Every young girl in a working-class family, like John's sister Mary Jane, worked to add to the family income. "The wages of the family's daughters were crucial to working class family subsistence," according to Philip S. Foner in *Women and the American Labor Movement*. Families needed their financial contributions, no matter how meager, to survive. Mary Jane was fortunate and was able to stop working when she married. Others were less able to do so despite their marital status.

Some men, like John's married co-worker Elias Sturges of New Brunswick, stayed behind in the factory when the war began. "I wrote a letter to Sturges." John reported to his mother in October 1861, "to get Jim Furlong and me a pipe and match box [items that Meyer manufactured] and give them to you to send and if he charges anything for them, let me know so that I can see how patriotic he is."

For many of the men who remained working in the factory, the exodus of male employees meant promotion. Robert Stewart, a year older than John, worked in the Button Shop. The Brunswick Boys who returned to camp from furlough carried the news of Stewart's elevation (most likely to foreman); this was just enough to whet John's appetite. "Please let me know some of the news about the Button Shop," John wrote home in February 1864. "I hear Bob Stewart is a boss now." While John struggled with private's pay, the realization that some who stayed home, like Stewart, received a promotion along with more pay must have been a galling thought.

Still, the factory represented reliability for the Hamilton family. Once John was mustered out of the army and returned to New Brunswick, his skills were limited to what he did before the war; certainly, army skills were not easily transferable to postwar life. John likely returned to Meyer, at least for the short term, in order to help the family financially, as did many of the other Boys. Until they were assimilated into civilian life and started new career paths with greater opportunities for advancement, the factory was an environment they knew. The war also taught them common lessons: life was tenuous, and if they were to succeed, they realized that it would be by their own drive and determination.

Camp near Brandy Station, Virginia
Feb. 16, 1864

Dear Mother,

I take this opportunity to inform you that I am well and hope this finds you the same. I received your letter day before yesterday also the fine comb, postage stamps and silk handkerchief. I have got the first one you sent me yet and the second one you sent me I have never used so I am pretty well off for handkerchiefs for I also have a white linen one.

I received a letter from Aleck not long ago. He was still at Chattanooga and expects to stay there all summer. He was in good health and they are getting full rations now for the first time since they were there.

The men who re-enlisted from our battery and went home on furlough will be back tomorrow night and I think they wont be quite as happy as they were when they went away.

I am glad you received the locket all right. It is not worth much but the picture will show you about how I look. I suppose you dont have to pay as much for a picture as I did. For that it cost $1.50. I think you could get a locket like that and picture too for that much money but it wont be long now before I will be home where I can buy things at white men's prices.

I dont know any more news at present so I will close.

With love to all. Remember me to all enquiring friends.

From your afectionate son,
John

Camp near Brandy Station, Virginia
Feb. 23rd, 1864

Dear Mother,

I take this opportunity of informing you that I am well and hope this finds you and yours the same. The Boys came back on the 19th and they say they had a fine time and I believe they had.

Those two men who were in Brunswick and stopped to see you and Furlong's father told me about it. They gave me the pipe you sent and tobacco and I am obliged to you. They told me that Susan is a large girl nearly as tall as men and Alice is also a fine girl. I suppose I will hardly know them when I get home and it wont be a great while now—if I am lucky—only 3 months.

The youngest one of those men who stopped to see you is a wild fellow but he acted sensible. When he was home he got married to a good steady country girl and left her a good home and piece of land. He bought it by paying a little over half cash down and the rest to be paid in installments, $20 at a time.

The men do not appear to be sorry they re-enlisted but they are satisfied they could have made out better home than they can out here at 13 dollars a month. So I think they wish now that they had stayed here until their time was out, but it is too late now and they will have to stay until the war is closed.

I hope the Rubber Company was not mean enough to charge you anything for that pipe. If they did, let me know and I will send it back to them. I will not use it until I hear from you for I expect I can get as good a pipe out here for the same money.

I dont know anything more of importance so I will close with my love to the girls.

From your afectionate son,
John

I have written to Aleck but have no answer yet.

Chapter 14
"No Furlough for You, Son"

Three more men left the battery on furlough for home. I am satisfied I will not get a furlough for the Captain gives the married men the preference and next to them comes his personal friends...I wish I could have got one before we commence this campaign but it is too late now and I don't believe any more will be given until next fall.
–April 16, 1863, White Oak Church, Virginia

Throughout the course of the war, many of John's friends and fellow soldiers received furloughs—some to marry sweethearts at home, many to mourn lost family members and still others to be comforted by family and friends. Friends on their leaves to New Brunswick often visited John's mother and sometimes Jim Furlong's father. John, who never received a furlough or left the theater of war, asked others to deliver or bring back important items for him.

After his younger brother's death, John asked Sailor Bill to return James Hamilton's personal belongings to Mrs. Hamilton on his leave. John Vroom was entrusted to return to camp with a photograph of John's mother and sisters. Others performed similar tasks, returning to camp with tobacco, pipes and other items sent by family. If John could not get a furlough for himself, then his friends, who reenlisted and received a furlough as a "bonus," could act as his surrogate when they visited home.

Furloughs were given by a commander who was quartered with the soldier's company or regiment. It was a discretionary process that was often abused. A furloughed soldier was required to carry papers with a detailed physical description, departure and return dates, unit designation and pay allowance. The papers warned the soldier to rejoin his unit by a specific date "or be considered a deserter."

In his letter to his mother, John explained that his commanding officer first gave furloughs to the married men in the unit and then to his own friends. It wasn't likely that John would get one. Even when his father was desperately ill in late 1863, he wrote to his mother that "I think it is almost impossible."

When John received a letter from his sister in January 1863 reporting his father's sharp decline in health, he took the letter to Lieutenant Augustine N. Parsons, the commander of the battery (he served in the absence of the captain), and requested a furlough. Lieutenant Parsons "told me he could do nothing. The other the day the Orderly Sergeant got a letter from home telling him his two children were very sick and not expected to live. The lieutenant tried all he could to get a furlough for him, but it was no use. Letters of that kind come very often and the officers are getting sick of them."

Influence, on the other hand, John opined, might be one way to receive a furlough. "About the only way I could get one," he wrote in January 27, 1863, "would be for you to go to some influential man in New Brunswick and get him to see the Governor. I think John B. Hill would be a good man to go to. I think if the Governor knew that Father was dying of his wounds and wanted to see me, he could manage it."

Hill, a former New Brunswick mayor from 1853 to 1855, was a person of influence in New Jersey politics. Unfortunately, it is doubtful that Mrs. Hamilton ever had a chance to see him. John's father died the day after John wrote his letter.

There was, of course, one confirmed method of receiving a furlough: reenlist. During the winter of 1863–64, the Union army was desperate for reenlistments. The patriotic enthusiasm from the start of the war had waned considerably, and the unpopular draft movement was not nearly as successful as anticipated. In the North, federal, state and local bounty systems were initiated.

Begun in May 1861 the federal system offered $100 to three-year volunteers and regulars. For those who reenlisted two years later in 1863, the sum had grown to $300. By early 1864, the bounty had reverted to $100, until the $300 was restored in July of that year. To sweeten the process, a thirty-day furlough was given to soldiers willing to sign on for three more years. "We had an order read to us this morning," John wrote on December 23, 1863, "for re-enlisting for 3 years or during the war a big bounty and 30-days furlough was offered."

Bounty programs varied from state to state, from regiment to regiment and even according to the enlistee's marital status or race. Some enlistment and reenlistment programs offered lucrative bounties, while others provided nominal amounts. A few states offered property in lieu of cash bounties. New Jersey, like other Union states, used recruitment and enrollment posters to advertise for men. In some New Jersey regiments, like the Twelfth, a bounty of $266 was offered to married men for enlistment ($222 for single men) plus an additional $100 bounty from the federal government. Such cash bounties were tempting inducements that many soldiers accepted. There was much a soldier could do with $300 in the 1860s.

When one of John's friends returned home on thirty-day leave after reenlisting, he married "a good steady country girl and left her a good home and piece of land. He bought it by paying a little over half cash down and the rest to be paid in installments, $20 at a time." The $300 bounty he received must have gone a long way toward wedding expenses and the house.

As much as John wanted to come home to see his family after his father's death, he was resigned to staying for the duration. He did not choose to reenlist. "I will come home first," he told his mother, "and see how I can get along and then, if I want to go again, I can probably get a big bounty."

Camp near Brandy Station, Virginia
Dec. 23rd, 1863

Dear Sister Susan,

I received your letter yesterday and was glad to hear from you. There is snow on the ground this morning. It is the first we have had of any account. I suppose by the time this reaches you, it will be Christmas and I hope you will all enjoy it and New Year's also. If I were home I would give you all some nice presents but out here I cannot buy anything for you so I will send a little money for you and Alice to buy something for yourselves. I would send you more if I had it. So I will just divide what I have between you and Alice and I hope you will enjoy it. You can buy more with this than I could out here with 5.00 dollars.

This will get to you before New Year's I hope and if it does, you and Alice can go down town and buy something nice and it will be the same as if I were there and gave it to you. That is if you can only think so.

I can remember the last New Year's Day that I was home very well. I started from home in the morning with a new overcoat on and Jim Furlong and his brother were with me and all had overcoats alike and we had a jolly day, but when I came home I will have a holy day of my own and maybe it will be as good as the 4th of July. No more at this time.

Give my regards to all friends and love to Alice and Mother and I wish you all a happy Christmas and New Year.

From your afectionate brother,
John

Direct your letters John Hamilton, 1st N.J. Art. Battery A, care of Capt. Hexamer's Artillery Reserve, Army of Potomac

Dear Mother,

I must write you a few lines as I have space left. I wrote you a letter the other day which I suppose you have received before this. If you have, you have seen the reason why I did not send you any money last pay day. If you have sent me a box, I guess I will get it all right for we are in winter quarters now and if anything is directed right it stands a pretty good chance of coming through all right. I hope nobody will open it and take out the mince pies. I have not forgotten the ones you sent me when we were at Camp Seminary near Alexandria.

I suppose you remember little Martin Connolly who used to drill buttons in the factory. He came out here as private in the 55th New York. He was promoted to color bearer for bravery and at the Battle of Antietam was wounded in four different places while carrying the flag, but he brought the colors out with him at the Battle of Chancellorsville. He also distinguished himself and was promoted to Quartermaster Sergeant and has since been promoted to 2nd Lieutenant. I saw him day before yesterday. He is only 18 years old now. He had made out better than any of the New Brunswick boys and it is all owing to his bravery for when he enlisted he was a stranger to all of his comrades and officers but I do not appear to have any such luck.

We had an order read to us this morning for re-enlisting for 3 years or during the war. A big bounty and 30 days furlough was offered but I will come home first and see how I can get along and then, if I want to go again, I can probably get a big bounty.

No more this time.

From your faithful son,
John

Camp near Brandy Station, Virginia
Jan. 27th 1864

Dear Mother,

I received your letter and was glad to hear you were all well. In regard to getting a furlough I think is almost impossible. About the only way I could get one would be for you to go to some influential man in New Brunswick and get him to see the Governor. I think John B. Hill would be a good man to go to. I think if the Governor knew that Father was dying of his wounds and wanted to see me, he could manage it.

I shall have to stop or I will not get this off in this mail. No more at present.

From son,
John

Camp near Brandy Station, Virginia
Jan. 28th, 1864

Dear Mother,

I received a letter from you last night and was sorry to hear that Father was worse. I took the letter up and showed it to Lieutenant Parsons who is commander of the Battery in the absence of the Captain and asked him if he could get me a furlough to go home and see him and he told me he could do nothing. The other day the Orderly Sergeant got a letter from home telling him his two children were very sick and not expected to live. The lieutenant tried all he could to get a furlough for him, but it was no use. Letters of that kind come very often and the officers are getting sick of them.

We have not 225 men and it is rumored that some of the men whose time is nearly out will be sent home to save keeping them over the winter but I guess it is all talk. We have not much longer to serve now and the time flies pretty fast.

I hope Father will live to see me come home. I have tried all I know how to get home to see him and that is all I can do without I desert and I guess he would not want to see me do anything like that nor would you.

I have something to send Susan. I will send it in your name. We may not see another battle before my time is out but if we do, I will try and dodge the balls as I have sometimes done before. You may laugh at the idea, but I am satisfied that if have never done any dodging, I would be a head shorter than I am now.

I hope Aleck will have better luck getting a furlough than I had. Give my love all.

Your afectionate son,
John

Camp near Brandy Station, Virginia
Jan. 29, 1864

Dear Mother,

I write you to let you know I am well and I received a letter from Mary Jane last night.

She told me about Father's death. I did not expect it but death comes when we least expect it. I am very sorry I could not have come home and seen him before he died.

I can remember very well the last time I saw him. It was on the 7 days retreat to Harrison's Landing. I think it was on the 2nd day, he was wounded at the Battle of Fair Oaks. He had been in an ambulance but they put him out to make room for men who were wounded so bad that they could not get along at all. He had a stick or crutch he had cut in the woods and was getting along the best he could. The next morning we moved again and I kept with him as long as I could. He could not get along very fast so we got behind and when our rear guard came along they made me leave him and hurry ahead and join my regiment so I had to shake hands with him and leave him in the rear.

Dear Mother, I do not think it is worth while to bother any more getting a furlough now for it will cost a good deal of money and I have not much longer to serve now. Dont fail to use my money to pay any expenses there will be to bury Father in good shape.

I sent Susan a small locket with my picture in it yesterday. I found it some time ago and was agoing to send it to her for a New Years present but I did not have the money to have the picture taken but I sold my watch for 10 dollars. It would not run so it was no use to me. Tell Alice she must not be jealous of Susan because I sent her the locket. I sent it to her because she is the oldest.

Please send me a few postage stamps in your next. No more at present.

From your son,
John

P.S. Please let me know some of the news about the Button Shop. I hear Bob Stewart is a boss now.

Chapter 15

A Bittersweet Homecoming

I have not received any letter from you in about 2 months and I feel very anxious for the last time I heard from you, you were not well.

–May 13, 1864, camp near Salem Heights, Virginia

Although the war had almost a year before its end, John's return to New Brunswick in June 1864 was bittersweet. By the time he was mustered out, his father, Alexander, was dead, along with his dreams of purchasing a farm for the family in Pennsylvania; younger brother James, who had been so eager to go to war, lay in an unmarked grave at Bullock's Farm in Spotsylvania, Virginia, while older brother Aleck, still in the Nineteenth Indiana Regiment, was marching through Tennessee and Georgia fighting.

To make matters worse, in April, two months before John was to be discharged, he learned that his mother was ill. After receiving the news of her illness, he did not hear from her for another two months. His sisters Mary Jane, Susie and Alice also did not write. Perhaps their mother asked them not to worry John with her illness and forbade them to do so.

John's worst fear was that he might not return in time to see his mother alive. Just a few months earlier, he had told his mother, when he was unsuccessful in getting a furlough to see his dying father, that the only possibility was to get someone influential, like former New Brunswick mayor John B. Hill, to intervene with the governor.

Certainly, John felt guilty for not returning in time to see his father, and it weighed on him. "I am very sorry I could not have come home and seen him before he died." Then he was presented with the news that his mother was ill. "Dear Mother," he wrote in April 1864, "if you get ill, let me know at once and if there is any possible way for me to get home to see you without deserting, I will come. You remember when you wrote to me about Father being so low. Well I received the letter the same night he died so I would not have seen him alive if I had got a furlough."

Imagine John's frustration in not hearing from his sick mother and his haste to return home as soon as possible. Just a month before his discharge, he wrote, "I feel very anxious for the last time I heard from you, you were not well so I am watching for a letter from you every day and dont get any."

What awaited John in New Brunswick, besides an ill mother and a broken family in mourning, were John's friends who had returned from the war, some wounded and disabled and others in coffins to be buried by their families.

Then, just before John was to be discharged, he came across his New Brunswick friend, Lieutenant Benjamin Moffett, in a hospital tent at Locust Grove in Virginia, where doctors had amputated his leg.

Having sustained his injury in the Battle at Wilderness in May 1864, Moffett sadly died within days of his meeting with John. Another Brunswick Boy was more fortunate. Mary Jane's friend, Ike DeForrest, was given a disability discharge in early 1863 and sent to a convalescent camp in Virginia after sustaining his injury before returning home.

While many of the Boys had sustained external physical injuries or wounds that lasted their lives, they also had experienced the violence of war, which left an even deeper mark. Yet despite these injuries and suffering and the overall disruption to life, there was obviously great joy at their return home. In June 1863, when Sailor Bill (William Stroud) and Bill Furlong, Jim's brother, were discharged, John wrote, "Furlong is glad for I never saw anybody want to get home as bad as he did."

When John and Jim Furlong finally mustered out in June 1864 at a camp near Petersburg, Virginia, there was little doubt that they returned to New Brunswick for a glorious homecoming. John marched straight to the family home on George Street in New Brunswick, where his mother, recuperating from a long illness, and his sisters Alice and Susan with Mary Jane (who had traveled from Newark) most likely greeted him with a warm and tender welcome. Jim Furlong presumably returned to an equally earnest welcome from his father, John, sisters Mary and Ann and recently returned brother William. Neither John nor Jim had seen his family for three long years.

Tents of a general hospital at City Point, Virginia, similar to the ones that Lieutenant Benjamin Moffett was taken to for treatment at Locust Grove. *Library of Congress.*

After a short respite at home, John realized that he needed to return to the rubber factory for work. While the company's work records are nonexistent, there is no question that he did so. His mother and two sisters at home were depending on his income and whatever Aleck could send. When Aleck was discharged in November 1864, he did not return to Indiana but instead traveled to New Brunswick to help John with family responsibilities.

As the oldest brother and the one who had been absent from the family in Indiana for several years before the war, Aleck must have felt a great emotional and financial obligation to help his mother and sisters after the death of his father, the death of his youngest brother and loss of their respective incomes. Despite the tragedies that the war had wrought, the reunion between the brothers and their family produced great happiness after the long separation of war. Unfortunately, their joy was short-lived. Tragically, a short year later, the oldest Hamilton sister, twenty-eight-year-old Mary Jane Hamilton Fouratt, suddenly became ill and died on December 22, 1865.

Mary Jane's death certificate listed peritonitis, an inflammation of the abdominal cavity membrane, as the cause of death. This massive infection can

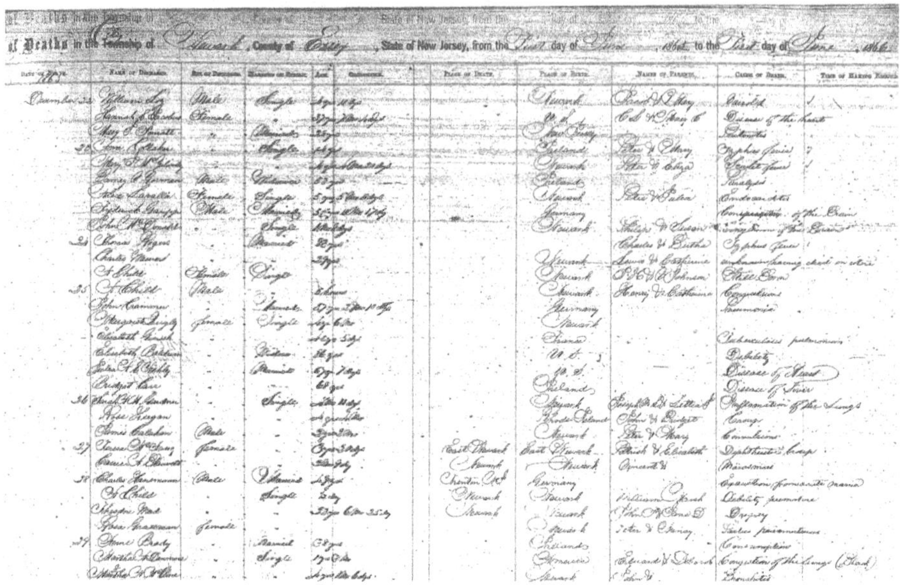

The death certificate of Mary Jane Hamilton Fouratt showed the cause of death as peritonitis, a not uncommon ailment at that time. *New Jersey State Archives, Department of State.*

be caused by a rupture, such as appendicitis or peptic ulcer, or might have been a byproduct of childbirth, although no record of a second child's birth could be located. Despite a diligent search, no records could be found to substantiate how she contracted peritonitis. Mary Jane left behind a four-year-old child, Mary Ida, and a bereft husband, mother, sisters and brothers.

John was twenty-one in 1865, and brother Aleck was twenty-three. When the war essentially ended in April 1865 with General Lee's surrender, the Hamilton boys looked forward to their future. They aspired to better wages than the rubber factory offered and needed higher incomes to support their mother and sisters, as well as themselves. Aleck, trained as a carpenter in Illinois, was likely the one to suggest that they open a carpenter shop in New Brunswick.

Soldiers were now returning home to their families and others to marry and start new families. There was to be an economic boom in the North, with new railroad building, more industry and expanding commerce. Wages finally were increasing, and former soldiers needed consumer goods, furniture and dwellings. Carpentry was to become a thriving business in postwar New Brunswick. So, pooling their savings, Aleck and John opened a carpentry business in 1866.

Mar 9th, 1864

Dear Mother:

Yours of the 21st came to hand 4 days ago and I was glad to hear from you. It is raining here to day so I thought I would sit down and write to pass the time away. We have been paid since my last and I sent you 15 dollars by the paymaster. We have been mustered for the last 2 months pay and expect to get it in a week or so and then I think I can send you 15 more.

I bought me a vest and a cap this pay day. I paid 5 dollars for the vest and 2½ for the cap.

Yesterday two men left here for home on 30 days furlough. They re-enlisted. One of them is from New Brunswick. His name is John Vroom. He married on of those Stilwell girls, sister of Sarah Stilwell who used to work in the button factory. He promised to call and see you before he came back. If he does I wish you would send me a picture of Susan, Alice and you taken in one picture. The picture you sent me of yours I have got yet but it is spoiled. It got wet and dirty and in trying to clean it, I about destroyed it but I am a going to try and keep it for a relic to put on the mantel piece. I always carried it in my pocket. If I had not, it would have been gone long ago as I have lost at least 5 knapsacks since I was out here.

One man in our battery had his life saved by having a likeness in his pocket at Gettysburg. He was wounded in 3 places by shrapnel. Shell exploded near him and one of the balls went through his arm, another through his thigh. The third hit him in his breast pocket and through 8 letters and his wife's picture and made a bruise over his heart. He is in Trenton now or was the last I heard from him.

It is very lonesome in camp when it rains. When it is pleasant, we play ball and have a good time but such weather as this, we write, play cards or lay around the tent and snore.

I have not heard from Aleck in some time. I got a letter from Mary Jane the other day. Give my love to Susan and Alice and remember me to all enquiring friends.

From your afectionate son,
John

Camp near Brandy Station, Virginia
April 23rd, 1864

Dear Mother,

I received yours of the 19th last night and was sorry to hear you were not well and I hope this will find you better. I guess you have not received the last two letters I sent you. In one I put 5 dollars bill and the other a 20 dollar bill, but I suppose you have received them by this time.

Dear Mother, I want you to use the money I send home for you and the girls. When I come home I dont want to find out that you could have used it for your comfort and had not done it. If you don't do anything else with it, buy good things to eat and buy the best of porter for yourself to drink.

You remember when I worked for Sammy March, the baker. His wife used to send me to the drug store nearly everyday for a bottle of brown stout porter and I suppose that is what made her so healthy.

I see by your letter that you think I will have to stay here until the 27th of June but they think that we will be discharged on the 6th as our old company was mustered into the United States service on the 6th of June 1861. Of course my 3 years are not up until June 26, 1864 and I may not get discharged until then but it is only 20 days anyway and that will soon pass.

You spoke in your letter about Major Fourall. He has been promoted to Colonel and transferred to the 33rd N.J. and they are in the south western army with Sherman.

Dear Mother, if you get very sick let me know at once and if there is any possible way for me to get home to see you without deserting, I will come. You remember when you wrote to me about Father being so low, well I received that letter the same night he died so I would not have seen him alive if I had got a furlough.

Several of the batterys that have been in camp near us all winter have left their camps and joined different army corps. We have not received any orders yet but we are all ready to get out of camp at short notice.

I dont know any more news so I will close with my love to the girls. Hoping to hear that you are perfectly well when you write again, I remain,

Your afectionate son,
John

Camp near Salem Heights, Virginia
May 13th, 1864

Dear Mother,

I have just found out that we have got a chance to send a letter so I will write. I am well and hope this finds you the same. We broke camp 10 days ago[1] *and there has been fighting every day since we left camp. Our battery has not been engaged yet. The country we are fighting through is so thick with woods that the artillery does not have much chance to get to work so the infantry has had to do most of the fighting.*

I saw Lieutenant Moffit in a hospital tent at Locust Grove. The doctors had just taken his leg off. Major Way was there also, wounded in the head. The 1st New Jersey is pretty well cut up I hear and I guess if I had stayed in that Regiment, I would have stopped a bullet before this time for there are not many there but have been hit.

I have not received any letter for you in about 2 months and I feel very anxious for the last time I heard from you, you were not well so I am watching for a letter from you every day and dont get any. There has been but one mail to us since we left Brandy Station but you must write to me and I will get it as soon as there is a chance for the mail to come through.

We have captured about 15,000 prisoners and 42 pieces of artillery. They are 5,000 prisoners near us now and they are getting them in line to take to the rear.

Give my love to Susan and Alice.

Your affectionate son,
John

P.S. When you write to Mary Jane, tell her I get her papers regularly and will write to her as soon as my finger gets well

1. On May 4, the Union Army of the Potomac crossed the Rapidan River to attack the Confederate Army of Northern Virginia. By May 13, the Battle of the Wilderness had been fought, and fighting was continuing at Spotsylvania Court House.

Chapter 16

Hamiltons at Home

When Johnny comes marching home again Hurrah! Hurrah!
We'll give him a hearty welcome then Hurrah! Hurrah!
The men will cheer and the boys will shout The ladies they will all turn out
And we'll all feel gay When Johnny comes marching home.
—*"When Johnny Comes Marching Home," written by Patrick Gilmore, 1863*

With the Hamilton family together again in New Brunswick, life became more predictable. John and Aleck worked diligently to support themselves, their remaining two sisters and their mother. At some point, they also must have thought about starting families of their own.

The first of the Brunswick Boys to marry after the war was John's best friend and wartime companion, Jim Furlong, who in December 1865 married Ellen Dugel in New Brunswick. Ellen was just sixteen, and Jim was twenty-two, not an unusual age difference for the time. For a young man away from home and family for three years, it must have been comforting to find a wife to settle down with in anticipation of permanency.

Two years later, after a passionate and robust courtship, John married Lydia Jane Howland on August 27, 1867, at the First Presbyterian Church in Red Bank. Reverend Charles E. Hill performed the ceremony, and their parents, siblings and a few close friends were in attendance. Lydia Howland—or Lida Jane, as she was sometimes known—was descended from a humble but well-established family who traced their ancestry to Henry Howland of Plymouth, Massachusetts, brother to John Howland (who arrived on the *Mayflower*;

Henry arrived in New England a year later). In October of that year, just a few months after their marriage, the Hamiltons' first child, Minnie, was born. Although their marriage could be viewed as legitimizing Lydia's pregnancy, there can be little doubt that theirs was a loving, long and fruitful marriage.

The following year, in 1868, Aleck married Irish-born Lizzie M. Silliland on January 18. The wedding was performed by Reverend A.V. Lawrence, pastor of the First Methodist Church on Liberty Street in New Brunswick, and it is likely that the immediate Hamilton family attended.

With young families to support now, both Aleck and John worked long hours in the carpentry shop to maintain their own families, as well as to help support the home for their mother and two sisters.

John and Lydia welcomed a second child, Laura, in 1869. By then, John and his small family had moved to the corner of John and New Streets, while Aleck moved in 1870 to Mine Street, close to College Avenue, the present-day site of Rutgers University. Aleck's daughter, Jennie, was born a year later in 1870. The boys' mother, Mary Ann, continued to live at the family home with her daughters, Alice and Susan.

Alice, who turned eighteen in 1870, was the next to marry. She wed Miller Boudinot, a New Brunswick butcher, on January 4, 1870, and the young couple lived with Mary Ann in the family home on George Street. The happy event was a welcome relief to a family beset by still another tragedy.

Just months earlier, a family crisis occurred when on November 12, 1869, John's favorite sister, twenty-one-year-old Susan, who suffered from epilepsy as a child, was committed to New Jersey State Hospital, now Trenton Psychiatric Hospital. Although the commitment law was changing to allow voluntary admission, it is doubtful that Susan committed herself. After 1870, certificates of insanity signed by physicians were regarded as essential for commitment, and it is likely that one was issued for Susan.

Mary Ann accompanied her daughter to the hospital. The admitting documentation provided a brief history. Susan was subject to epilepsy when young, but the report noted that she had had no fits since she was ten years old. While epilepsy can, in fact, remain dormant for many years, this medical fact had not been discovered at the time Susan was admitted.

The overall symptom Susan presented was "crying violently at times." She also told the admitting officer that "her heart had stop beating." She was reported quiet of late and speaking seldom, "keeps in bed at night and is cleanly in habits with good bodily health." A considered cause was "self abuse," which Mary Ann told the hospital officials her daughter practiced some years ago, although she provided no examples.

While it is impossible to diagnose Susan based on the limited information at hand, it appeared that she suffered from severe depression and was deeply disturbed, as her medical records demonstrate. Ironically, her symptoms, while serious, far exceeded those needed for a woman's admittance to a psychiatric hospital in the 1860s.

The symptoms that qualified a woman's admittance at that time included such things as depression after the death of a loved one, use of inappropriate language and lack of a menstrual cycle, among others—symptoms that today certainly would not be grounds for admittance to a psychiatric institution. Again, afflictions like epilepsy, which today are treated with drugs, were not well understood at the time.

Thus, it was relatively easy for a husband or a father to have a wife or daughter committed to an institution on rather flimsy grounds. Certainly, it is likely that it enabled some men to remove an irksome spouse or troublesome child from their home, perhaps to "teach" the unruly one some acceptable behavior.

Susan's history and circumstances were ones of profound loss. She was now the oldest living unmarried daughter, she suffered the violent loss of her father and brother in war and her oldest sister from a massive infection within a few years, her beloved brother John married and moved from home and her brother Aleck also married and lived elsewhere. Now her younger sister, Alice, was about to be married as well, even though she was living at the family home. Taken together, these staggering emotional events within a short time span might have precipitated an emotional breakdown, or at the least a serious depression.

Whatever the reasons, Susan's admittance was significant for several reasons. New Jersey State Hospital was a state-of-the-art facility, founded just twelve years earlier by reformer Dorothea Dix. It was the first institution of its kind established in New Jersey for the mentally ill and the first in the country designed on the Kirkbride Plan, a system of design for mental asylums founded by Philadelphia psychiatrist Thomas Story Kirkbride. He held that the architectural design of a facility and its comfort, privacy and ease were conducive to the progress of good mental health.

Prior to its establishment, the mentally ill were often confined at home, where they were separated from the rest of the family and visitors and sometimes locked in attics or cellars. In many other cases, they were even sent to jails or almshouses, county-run poorhouses that were the dumping ground for the intellectually disabled, destitute, aged and mentally ill. Treatment at the new hospital, however, included medicine, baths, exercise, regulation of diet and, as a last resort, forms of mechanical restraints.

New Jersey State Hospital, now Trenton Psychiatric Hospital, was a model for compassionate care of the emotionally disturbed. *Trentonian, Local History and Genealogy Collection, Trenton Public Library.*

John Hamilton Jr., the author's great-grandfather, was born in 1872. He was about five in this photo. *Author's collection.*

Susan stayed at the hospital from November 1869 through December 1, 1873, and the periodic three-month hospital reports documented in her file paint a troubled hospitalization. At one point, restraints were required "on account of a persistent habit of biting and picking her fingernails with pins keeping them sore." The words "quite demented" were used to describe her situation over and over, although the term "demented" was not defined.

On December 1, 1873, Susan was removed from the hospital by county authorities. We do not know the reason, but we can speculate that her mother may have been ill, or near death, and wanted her daughter by her side. There is good reason to suspect that Mary Ann had died by 1875, although after an exhaustive search, no records of her death can be located. Her son Aleck and her daughter Alice, with their families, left the area in 1875, and it is unlikely that they would have moved, especially far away, if Mary Ann were alive.

The records show that in 1876 Susan was readmitted to the New Jersey State Hospital, but the hospital records are either incomplete or missing for that period. After a thorough search of hospital and state death records (inmates were buried with numbers, not names on their grave markers; numbers had to be correlated to a code book to identify names and Susan's name was not found), no record of Susan's death can be located. The circumstances of Susan's death and final resting place are a mystery.

Meanwhile, the Hamilton family was flourishing. Alice and Miller had a daughter, Mary A., in 1871. That same year, Aleck and Lizzie had a second daughter, Lizzie. Aleck and John's family lived together at Mine Street near College Avenue at least from 1870 to 1871. John moved from the house in 1872 to the corner of John and New Streets, where John Jr. was born that same year. Another baby, William, son of Aleck and Lizzie, joined the family in 1872. The following year, in 1873, John and Lydia had their fourth child, Edna.

The Hamiltons were growing by leaps and bounds, and the carpentry business was good, until Aleck, struck again by wanderlust, decided to move west. John, who reconnected to Aleck because of the war, was about to lose him again. In 1875, Aleck and his family, along with his sister Alice and her family, moved west to Detroit, Michigan, where the Boudinots may have still had relatives (records show that Miller's sister, Ella, was born in Michigan before the family moved to New Jersey).

John struggled to keep the carpentry shop open without Aleck, but by 1877, when baby Ida arrived, he decided to specialize and became a sash and blind maker. Business was poor, and the family was in dire straits. Brother

Aleck, now settled in Detroit, wrote to John with glowing reports of the city situated on the west bank of the Detroit River, across from the Canadian town of Windsor. Detroit was a town, he told his brother, where the streets were sixty to one hundred feet wide and lined with rows of trees. A small city population—just over 100,000—made the city feel open and free.

Then, too, the city was developing a reputation, along with Cedar Rapids, as the furniture capital of the nation—a great location for carpenters like Aleck and John. By 1890, the state employed some seven thousand people in 178 furniture factories across the region.

While machine production of furniture reduced prices by decreasing the amount of hand labor to build a price of furniture, machines could not do all the work. An extremely skilled craftsman may have earned up to seven dollars per day. By working sixty to seventy hours per week, it was possible to bring home the unheard-of amount of seventy dollars per week. Aleck urged John to leave New Jersey and come to Detroit.

By 1878, John and his family had moved to Detroit to join the rest of the family, but the only work he could find was as a "drayman," driving a low flatbed wagon to transport goods. That same year, John and Lydia had another child, Sylvester. It must have been unsettling for John and his wife to uproot their family, incur the expense of moving west and disrupt their life. With the newest addition to the family and the lack of a substantial income to sustain them, John decided to return the family to New Jersey, settling in Long Branch to be closer to his wife's family in a mid-sized city where, hopefully, there were better opportunities.

The Hamilton family was scattered. Father Alexander and brother James were dead. Sister Mary Jane was gone, too, and Susan had been recommitted to the asylum. Aleck and Alice were settled in Detroit with their families. Even Jim Furlong, John's best friend, had moved to Morris County in north Jersey to find better employment. The family was hither and yon, and the Brunswick Boys, once strong and united, were pulling their lives together even as they dispersed.

Chapter 17

The Brunswick Boys

The growing age and infirmities of the old soldiers have made this institution practically a hospital. The men are unable to scrub floors, wash windows and wait upon each other.

–Disabled Soldiers Home Board of Managers Report, *Kearny, New Jersey, 1913*

Each of the Brunswick Boys returned to New Brunswick with hopes and dreams for peace, prosperity and family, but the world they returned to was far different from the one they left at the start of the war. The Civil War changed America significantly in its concept of self, its social fabric, its economic basis and even in the birth of new technology.

With the emancipation of slaves and the movement of women into more roles outside the home during the war, the old social order eroded. The war produced a new national sense of one country as opposed to a concept of the country as a collection of states, and the federal government and its laws gained supremacy for the first time. Technology in the form of new methods of warfare and transportation improvements with railroad construction opened new industries and the country to young men looking for adventure and opportunity.

Despite the changes to the country as a whole, it was still not easy to move very far from your roots. Returning veteran and Brunswick Boy Charlie Banks was no different in his dreams than the rest of the veterans. Before the war, English-born Charlie worked as a porter in a store, a person

Brunswick Boy Charlie Banks (seated bottom row, second from left, with a bowler hat) revisited the Gettysburg Battlefield in 1888 for a dedication. *New Jersey State Archives, Department of State.*

who greeted customers and carried packages. The job held little chance for advancement. Upon his return to New Brunswick, Charlie struck out into new ventures, trying his luck as a laborer and jeweler, but he met with little success. He married in about 1867 and eventually had two sons, Henry and Walter. In 1872, he was employed as a janitor for the New Brunswick Public Schools. By 1877, Banks had been promoted to sexton and janitor for the New Brunswick lower schools; he became the janitor for the high school in 1880. For many years, he lived on Liberty Street with his family before moving to Welton Street near Livingston Street about the time of his promotion in 1877. He lived there for the balance of his life.

Charlie never forgot the war or the Brunswick Boys with whom he served. In 1888, he returned to the Gettysburg Battlefield with fifteen men and women; together, they dedicated a monument to honor Battery B, First New Jersey Light Artillery, Third Corps.

After his first wife died, Banks married for a second time in 1895. In 1911, Banks died and was buried at Elmwood Cemetery in New Brunswick.

The other Brunswick Boys faced many of the same choices that confronted Charlie Banks: return to their old jobs, if they still existed, or strike out into new ventures. Another Brunswick Boy, Tommy Corrigan, wounded in the hand and neck and a prisoner in the infamous Andersonville Prison for nine months, survived to return to New Brunswick and marry Sarah McLane in 1869. Their son, William, was born in 1871.

An apprentice carpenter before the war, Tom worked as a carpenter for several years before changing professions to become a city policeman. His wife, Sarah, died in May 1879, and by 1880, the extended Corrigan family—his father John, seventy, and Tom's sisters and brothers—lived together with young William. Thomas died in 1925 and is buried at St. Peter's Cemetery in New Brunswick.

"Little" Martin Connelly, the button factory boy and John Hamilton's hero who ascended from color guard to second lieutenant, mustered out of Company A, Fifty-seventh New York Infantry, in July 1864. Martin settled in Brooklyn and married an Irish-born woman, Elizabeth. He worked as a laborer and had a son and daughter.

George Fouratt, who worked in the rubber factory along with his father, David, and who joined the army the same day with William Furlong, returned to the rubber factory and became a cutter, probably for boots. He lived at the family home at 132 Burnet Street for many years with his father, mother and siblings. Sometime in about 1865, the family moved to Newark's Seventh Ward, and George went to work for a different rubber company.

George met Mary Pierce from Caldwell, a few miles north of Newark, and they married in November 1873. By 1880, George had moved with Mary to New York City with their sons—Robert, five; Augustus, four; and baby George, two months old. George worked in still another rubber factory in the city.

Fouratt's boon companion in the war, William Furlong, stayed in New Brunswick. He married Catherine Moore after his return to New Brunswick in 1865. The couple had a son, John, born in 1868. William returned to the rubber factory and worked there for several years before "changing professions" to work in a cotton mill. In 1875, the couple had a daughter, Kathy. Catherine died in 1887. A resident of the Home for Disabled Soldiers in Kearny, New Jersey, at the same time as John Hamilton, William died in 1919 and is buried at Arlington Cemetery in Kearny.

William's brother, Jim Furlong, was John's best friend during the war. Discharged in June 1864 with John, he returned to New Brunswick, where he married Ellen Dugel of that city the following year. Ellen is believed to have died by 1870, and Furlong moved to Rockaway Township in Morris County,

New Jersey. He lived there with another brother, John; his sister-in-law, Jane; and their children: Margaret, John Jr. and Mary Jane. He and his brother worked as miners in the iron mines of north Jersey. By 1880, Jim had moved to Brooklyn, New York, and was working as a laborer, but he returned to Randolph in Morris County a few years later.

Jim never remarried and unfortunately suffered a debilitating stroke in 1894. Furlong, according to his medical application, was "helpless and able to walk but little." His physician, Dr. Stephen Pierson of Morristown, acted in place of a relative and was named as "friend" in the application to the New Jersey Home for Disabled Soldiers in Kearny. In a certificate of identification, part of the application for admission to the home, Lawrence Doyle, a fellow Irishman from New Brunswick, swore that he had known Furlong for thirty-three years. Furlong, who received no pension, was admitted to the Soldiers Home, where he died the following year at fifty-seven years of age. It was a sad and lonely end for John's best friend. Furlong is buried at Holy Sepulcher Cemetery in East Orange, New Jersey.

This "Stub" must not be used … ificate, but is to be kept by the physician, and … s convenience.

REPORT OF DEATH.

1. Full name of deceased James Furlong
2. Age Fifty Seven Years
3. Color White Occupation Laborer
4. Single, ~~married, widow or widower~~.
5 Country of birth Ireland
6 Last place of residence, Soldiers Home Kearny Hudson Co N. Jersey
7. How long resident in State
8. Place of death Soldiers Home Kearny Hudson Co N. Jersey
9. Father's name
Country of birth
10. Mother's name
Country of birth
11. Date of death July 17th 1895
Cause—Primary Cerebral apoplexy
Cause—Secondary
Mode of death (Clinical notes on opposite side.)
Length of sickness
Undertaker

Jim Furlong's death certificate listed the cause of death as apoplexy. Furlong died at fifty-seven years of age. *National Archives and Records Administration.*

The New Jersey Home for Disabled Soldiers, where many of the Brunswick Boys went at the end of their lives, was a home designed to operate with a minimum of paid help and maximum of veteran labor. There were actually two homes, one originally in Newark, Essex County, which moved to Kearny in New Jersey's Hudson County in 1888, and one in Vineland, Cumberland County, in far southern New Jersey (which opened in 1899). The veterans—or "inmates," as they were called—were expected to prepare meals, wait on tables, perform nursing duties in the hospital, clean the facilities and in general do all of the maintenance. Eventually, though, the realities of time caught up with the men.

In 1913, the board of managers reported, "Outside help should be substituted in most cases. The men now doing this duty average seventy years and should no longer be required to do the heavier work around the home." (If you were not ill or weary when you were admitted, you would soon be performing the chores necessary to run the home.)

John Tyler Lewis, another boon companion, returned to New Brunswick when he was mustered out in 1864 and married shortly thereafter. In 1867, he and his wife, Cornelia, had a son, Harry. John worked as a sailor or boatman for many years, and he and Cornelia spent their lives living in New Brunswick. John lived a long life, dying in 1922. He is buried at St. James Episcopal Church Cemetery in Piscatawaytown (now Piscataway), New Jersey.

Lewis's good friend was David Skillman, who joined up with John as a recruit the same day; the boys served together in the First New Jersey Regiment. David's father was a shoemaker like John and his father, but David worked as a machinist, probably in the rubber factory. He married Kate Taylor in September 1872, and they lived at 35 Carmen Avenue for many years. Like many of the Brunswick Boys, Skillman was admitted to the Soldiers Home in Kearny in 1890. He died in 1906 and was buried, like William Furlong, at Arlington Cemetery in Kearny.

Peter McGovern, one of the married men who served in the war, married Winifred Conner in New Brunswick just after the start of hostilities in May 1861. Their son, James, was born the same year. Peter had enlisted in the First New Jersey Regiment, Company F, and served until 1865, when he had been transferred into the Seventh Regiment, Company B, and promoted to sergeant. Two more sons, Peter and William, were born in 1864 and 1867.

For several years after the war, Peter remained in the U.S. Army and then worked as a laborer. He and his family lived on Codwise Avenue at the corner of Townsend during those years. Peter died in January 1880 and is

The Disabled Soldiers Home in Kearny became the final home for many of the Brunswick Boys, including John. *Kearny Museum.*

buried at St. Peter's Cemetery in New Brunswick. His wife, Winifred, filed for a widow's pension in 1883.

Another married man, Jarvis Wanser, enlisted and was promoted several times, mustering out as a captain of Company B, Fourteenth New Jersey Regiment. Married in 1858 to Sarah Britton, Jarvis worked as a bartender in his father's saloon business. When he returned to New Brunswick after the war, he opened an eating house called Capt. Jarvis Wanser Jr.'s Eating House on the corner of Hiram and Dennis Streets. By 1868, Jarvis had expanded the restaurant to include a billiard hall and also opened a bowling alley at 226 Burnet Street in 1870. He and his wife had two sons, Albert and Frank.

By 1880, Jarvis, who inherited from his landowner father, had saved a good deal of money, certainly more than enough to move from the city to the country. Wanser and his family relocated to Cumberland County in southwestern New Jersey, where he invested in real estate.

In 1899, when the Home for Soldiers in Vineland opened, Jarvis Wanser was confirmed as a member of its board of managers. He became the first commandant or superintendent of the New Jersey Veterans Memorial Home in Vineland in 1900 and served there until his death in 1908. Although most of the men of his regiment were confined to the Soldiers Home in Kearny, Wanser was in his element with his fellow soldiers. He is buried at Siloam Cemetery in Vineland.

Another good friend and working companion, Irish-born Michael Welsh, returned to New Brunswick the same month as John. Mike, who before the war worked in the rubber factory with John, returned there as a laborer. Only once did he try his hand at another career (in a saloon in 1870) before returning to work as a laborer. He lived on Bishop Street below George Street for many years. After 1887, the city directory no longer lists his whereabouts, and his fate remains unknown.

One of the "oldest" Brunswick Boys was John Vroom, a New Brunswick boatman or sailor who earned his living transporting people or cargo by boat on the Raritan Canal. Vroom enlisted in 1862 at the age of thirty-one. A private in the First New Jersey Light Artillery, Battery A, he married Julia Stillwell in about 1857, and they had a son, John, in 1857. Vroom returned to New Brunswick when he was mustered out in 1865 and lived out his years in the city. He died in 1895 and is buried at Van Liew Cemetery in New Brunswick.

Another New Brunswick boatman, Julius Meyers, with his brother, John, was the sole support of his widowed mother and five sisters when he enlisted in 1861. Jule returned to New Brunswick to work as a laborer, dying a decade later in 1875. He is buried at the Pitman Methodist Episcopal Cemetery in New Brunswick.

William Stroud, "Sailor Bill" to the other boys, returned home to work in a store. He married Harriet Longstreet in December 1863, and they had a daughter, Mary, by 1865. The 1900 census reported Stroud, who was then sixty-one years old, as working in a factory.

Active in the Grand Army of the Republic (GAR), a civil war veterans' organization, Stroud and his younger brother, John, were members of the Boggs-Janeaway GAR Post No. 67 in New Brunswick, an affiliate of the largest organization for Civil War veterans in the country. John, in fact, was a post commander. Founded in 1866, GAR linked men in their common experiences of war and also acted as an advocacy group in politics. Widowed by 1910, Stroud, like several of the other Brunswick Boys, lived at the Soldiers Home in Kearny until his death sometime after 1910.

All of the boys returned home to live productive lives, marrying, having children and working. Although New Brunswick boomed after the war and its population expanded, at heart it was a small town, and it is probable that the Boys stayed in touch, if not through work and social gatherings then through veterans' activities like with the GAR.

As William Shakespeare immortalized in *Henry V*, a "band of brothers" were the comrades who forged their loyalty in war, fighting together and surviving with the help of their brothers. Shakespeare wrote, "We few, we happy few, we band of brothers / For he that sheds his blood with me, shall be my brother."

The Brunswick Boys typified such a band of brothers who fought together, shed blood together and survived the bloodiest war in American history together—some to travel at the end to the same soldiers homes that cared for their comrades and others to be cared for by family members. As they grew older and passed away one by one, their contributions lived on in the memories of their friends and family.

Chapter 18

Family Man

In the way of entertaining amusement nothing has been left undone. The Long Branch Military Band of eighteen pieces is in attendance every evening and furnishes excellent music.

–New York Times, *December 20, 1895*

When Lydia and John Hamilton relocated to Long Branch on New Jersey's Atlantic coast in 1878, a distance of less than thirty-five miles from John's hometown of New Brunswick (with a short stopover in Detroit, Michigan), it might as well have been an entire continent away. The main transportation of the day, as in the war, was the railroad, and it would have been the Hamiltons' means of travel. While major cities and towns had cobblestones, brick or other improved surfaces, the roads between them were, at best, packed dirt and ill designed for long-distance travel, especially for a family with young children. Their journey to their new home must have been tiring at best.

Long Branch in 1880 was a posh resort for the wealthy, who traveled by train from New York and Philadelphia to enjoy the seashore, hotels, racetrack and casinos that proliferated in the ocean community. Ever since Mary Todd Lincoln visited in the early 1860s and President Ulysses S. Grant followed a few years later in the 1870s, the town had built on its reputation as a fashionable, sophisticated watering hole for the wealthy. Another attractive feature was the town's theaters, which often featured some of the greatest actors and actresses of the day.

A drawing of President Ulysses S. Grant's summer cottage in Long Branch. *From* Harper's Weekly, *August 1870.*

Seven U.S. presidents lived and vacationed at Long Branch, including James Garfield (who was brought to the city in hopes of recuperating after an assassin's bullet felled him in July 1888), Chester A. Arthur, Ulysses S. Grant, Benjamin Harrison, Rutherford B. Hayes, William McKinley and Woodrow Wilson. The "Hollywood of the East" also attracted the likes of actors Lillian Russell and Edwin Booth (the famous *Hamlet* actor and brother to John Wilkes Booth), artists and writers like Winslow Homer and Robert Louis Stevenson and, of course, scoundrels like Diamond Jim Brady and the adventuress and infamous beauty, Lily Langtry.

The Hamiltons were part of the working class that lived year round in Long Branch. When they arrived, John moved his family into a rental home on Jackson Street, north of Broadway. A few years later, he relocated the family to 504 Broadway, a charming clapboard house at the corner of Morrell Street, while he rented space to open a carpentry shop.

Actress Lillian Russell often vacationed in Long Branch. *Library of Congress.*

Soon, the family was expanding again as little Walter was born in 1881. But the following year once again brought tragedy to the family. The Hamiltons lost six-year-old Ida on December 4, 1882, and four-year-old Sylvester two days later. Both children were struck down with scarlet fever, then a serious childhood disease marked by the red rash that gave this terrible affliction its name. Its cause was a strep infection, and the survival rate before the discovery of antibiotics was abysmally low.

344
MILITARY
BAND
Great Grandfather John P. Hamilton
middle row—third from right.

HAYSEEDS

Alice—or Allie, as she was known—was born in 1884, but four years later, death struck the family again. Little Alice died from "paralysis of the heart" in 1888. According to her death notice, Alice "won all hearts by her patience and sweetness." The next year, the Hamiltons' last child, Jennie, was born. In all, there were nine children, six of whom survived childhood.

Besides working long days in his carpentry shop, John was active in the community. He was a member in the James B. Morris Post of the Grand Army of the Republic, No. 46, an affiliate of the national organization for Civil War veterans. The group met at the GAR Hall at 497 Broadway in Long Branch, and John was elected post commander in 1892, 1893 and again in 1896. The John B. Morris Post, named for Long Branch native James Morris, a first lieutenant with the First New Jersey Artillery, was one of the more active posts in the state, with a membership greater than fifty.

John also was an accomplished musician in the Long Branch Military Band. Although there are no documented records of his area of expertise, from the small area of the photograph with the band, it appears the instrument he played was a tenor tuba or euphonium, a brass instrument commonly used in concert and marching bands. The eighteen-piece band, housed at 563 Broadway, performed at all Long Branch ceremonial events.

In December 1895, the *New York Times* reported that the Industrial Exposition, the first of its kind in New Jersey, opened in Long Branch with great fanfare: "In the way of entertaining amusement nothing has been left undone. The Long Branch Military Band of eighteen pieces is in attendance every evening and furnishes excellent music. A concert commences every evening at 8 o'clock. The programme each night consists of ten well-selected numbers."

The band, with its wool uniforms of cap, dark jacket and pants, had a long history in the city. In August 1911, the *New York Times* reported again that the Military Band was an integral part of the children's or baby parade: "In all its interesting features the children's pageant surpassed last year's parade. The procession was made up of eleven divisions, headed by the Long Branch Military Band."

Opposite, top: John Hamilton (second row, third from right) played in the Long Branch Military Band. *Author's collection.*

Opposite, bottom: The "Little Hayseeds," Edna, sitting, and Herbert Hamilton, grandchildren of John, participated in the children's parade on the Boardwalk and won a prize. *Author's collection.*

John's own grandchildren, the children of John Jr. (John Herbert and Edna Mildred), often participated in the annual children's pageant or parade. On several occasions, they won awards for most "original costume and float," which were designed by their mother. In 1912 and 1913, their floats, entitled "Little Hayseeds" and "Our Emblem," not only won awards (silver-plated loving cups, which were large, two-handled cups often given as trophies) but also were photographed for posterity.

The early part of the twentieth century was busy for the old soldier, too, as John worked to expand his business. The Long Branch City Directory of 1896 listed John P. Hamilton Jr., John Sr.'s twenty-four-year-old son, as a carpenter who worked with his father. In 1900, father and son incorporated as J.P. Hamilton Jr. & Company. John Jr. also was given a second listing in the directory with "Isaac N. Cubberly, Stair Builders," located at Seventh Avenue and Broadway just down the street from their home on Broadway. In 1902, John Sr. moved back to Jackson Street, and he and his son and their families shared the house together.

A few years later, in 1904, John Jr. moved farther down the street to 49 Jackson Street with his young wife, the former Edna Haines. John Jr.'s success grew as he became a mason in Long Branch Lodge No. 78 of the Free and Accepted Masons. A few years later, he was even the proud owner of an automobile when few existed in 1911 Long Branch.

While John's family was establishing its roots firmly in New Jersey, it was not the same case with his brother. Aleck, who had moved to Detroit in 1874, continued his carpentry craft as his family expanded with the birth of a son, Alexander, the same year. Two years later, Elizabeth and Aleck's daughter Annie was born in 1878. Unfortunately, Annie died at age six in 1884.

Aleck's wanderlust propelled him, and following the dictum, "Go West, young man," he uprooted his family again to move to Washington State; by 1888, he was working in Seattle as a carpenter and living in various parts of the city until at least 1900. The Hamiltons lost two more children in Seattle: Jennie died in 1893, and Lizzie died in 1901. In 1904, Aleck and his wife relocated yet again to Los Angeles, California. Although a Home for Disabled Soldiers was established in Orting, Washington, in 1891, Aleck may have relocated to California to receive more extensive medical care than was available in Washington State, as he was quite ill.

Aleck was admitted to the U.S. National Home for Disabled Soldiers in Sawtelle, Los Angeles County, California, in December 1904 for chronic cystitis, a severely debilitating disease of the urinary bladder. At his own request, he was discharged on July 17, 1907, perhaps to spend his last few

Left: Like his father, John Hamilton's son, John Jr., worked as a carpenter and opened a successful contracting company. *Author's collection.*

Right: John Jr.'s wife, Edna, the former Edna Haines. *Author's collection.*

months at home before he died on April 1, 1908, a day short of his sixty-sixth birthday. Aleck was buried at the Los Angeles National Cemetery.

Elizabeth, Aleck's wife, remained in California and lived off her "own income," according to the 1910 Federal census; she took in a border, another senior matron. Her last known address was in Long Beach, California, in 1910, when she was sixty-five years old. Her son Alexander worked as a miner in Seattle, and unfortunately, her daughter Alice's whereabouts are unknown.

Alice and her husband, Miller Boudinot, had moved with Aleck and his family from New Brunswick to Detroit years before. The Boudinots had two more children in Michigan: James R., born in 1874 (who died in infancy), and Cecelia, who was born in 1877. Their older daughter, Mary A., her grandmother Hamilton's namesake, died at ten years of age in May 1881 in Detroit from "dropsy," an old term for edema or swelling of the soft tissue due to accumulation of water, which suggests congestive heart failure in modern terms.

Miller Boudinot, who worked as a policeman immediately after he moved to Detroit, returned to the butcher trade and was listed in the Detroit City Directory as such until 1882. Unfortunately, at that point in time, a new family mystery arises. After an exhaustive search, no records could be located for Miller or Alice after 1882, although daughter Cecelia and son William apparently relocated to New Jersey—Cecelia to Highland Park, next door to New Brunswick, to live with her aunt, Ella Boudinot Whitlock and her family through 1920. William moved to New Brunswick, where he is found listed in the 1910 directory. Cecelia never married and became a schoolteacher and then a principal in the public schools. William married a French immigrant, Louise, and worked as a salesman in a grocery store and also at a "government camp," according to census records, although the records do not specify where this camp was located. William died in 1940.

More death followed. Lydia Hamilton, John's beloved wife, grew ill and died in 1909 at age fifty-nine when her youngest child, Jennie, was just twenty years old. John was sixty-five years old, and he and Lydia had been married for forty-two years. Jennie went to live with her sister Edna and Edna's husband, Edward Haviland, in Manhattan, New York. Edward owned a fish and oyster store, and Jennie became his bookkeeper until her marriage to Harry Bolshaw of Brooklyn in 1910.

Although Jennie had two sisters who lived nearby—Minnie Hamilton Riddle in Eatontown, New Jersey (who had a twenty-year-old daughter and a thirteen-year-old-son), and Laura Hamilton Wooley of Long Branch, New Jersey (who had a seventeen-year-old son and an eleven-year-old daughter)—Jennie probably chose to live with Edna because Edna had lost her only daughter, Mildred, just a few years earlier. Although sixteen years separated them, Edna also was the sister closest in age to Jennie.

With Lydia's death, John's health declined dramatically. In May 1910, he made an application for admission to the New Jersey Home for Disabled Soldiers, where many of the Brunswick Boys now called home. The Home for Disabled Soldiers in Kearny, New Jersey, was one of the first established in the United States. The first home in the state opened in 1866 in Newark, but it was closed in 1888 and moved to Kearny, where several of the Brunswick Boys spent the last months and years of their lives.

The examining surgeon listed John's disability as a double hernia with general debility on the certificate of disability. A month later, the attending surgeon at the home added valvular disease of the heart, a disease process involving one or more valves of the heart, to his disability.

John's stay at the home was not without more family tragedy. In 1915, John's oldest son and namesake marched in the Long Branch Decoration Day Parade (now known as Memorial Day). It was a cold, wet day, and the forty-four-year-old came down with a severe cold. He died of pneumonia two weeks later, leaving a widow and two small children. My great-grandfather's heartbreak must have been wrenching.

We know, too, that John left the Home for Disabled Soldiers to stay with his daughter Laura in Long Branch in June 1918. Before he left Kearny for the final time, he signed his last will and testament in a strong hand, designating his oldest daughter, Minnie, as executrix. Ill and failing fast, he died at Laura and Harry Wooley's home on Norwood Avenue in Long Branch on Monday, July 15, 1918, at 5:30 p.m. of heart disease. He was seventy-four years old and had outlived his siblings and several children. He had survived the country's most destructive war during which, as a private, he fought in many battles, received several gunshot wounds and was honorably discharged. Like many soldiers of the past and today, he kept the haunting memories inside, unable to share the horror with those who were not there.

One of his lasting family legacies was that of John's only surviving son, Walter Asay Hamilton, who perhaps after his father's example of patriotism and service registered for World War I when he was thirty-six years old and then again in 1942 for World War II when he was sixty years old.

Laura and Minnie requested John's personal belongings from the home. The list included one overcoat, one vest, four colored shirts, one pair shoes, one pair slippers, one shaving outfit, letters and postal cards, four pair socks, miscellaneous articles, one suitcase and one small case. In a strange coincidence, the list paralleled the one John made for his mother in 1861 when he recorded his regimental belongings.

Both the *Red Bank Register* and the *Asbury Park Press*, the two area newspapers, reported John's death. The *Register* article was headlined, "Death of War Veteran, Long Branch Man Was in Many Battles in Civil War." It read, in part, "[Mr. Hamilton] enlisted almost at the start of the civil war and was in at least fifty battles. One of his three brothers in the army was killed and Mr. Hamilton's father was wounded in battle and died some time later."

However, no article or report of death could convey the camaraderie and brotherhood that John experienced with his fellow Brunswick Boys nor the lives and experiences they shared in the war. John's life was a rich tapestry of hard work, loving family and good friends. He and the Brunswick Boys left a legacy that lives beyond them through their contributions to their country, their families and, most of all, their loyalty to one another. They epitomized a band of brothers bound by blood. May they be at peace.

Appendix

The Brunswick Boys

Banks, Charles

- private, Company K, Third New Jersey Infantry Regiment, enlisted April 1861
- discharged July 1861
- reenlisted corporal, Battery B, First New Jersey Volunteer Light Artillery, September 1861
- discharged September 1864

Connelly, Martin R.

- private, Company A, New York Fifty-seventh Infantry, enlisted September 1861
- corporal, May 1862
- sergeant, January 1863
- quartermaster sergeant, June 1863
- reenlisted February 1864
- second lieutenant, Company C, March 1864
- discharged August 1864

Corrigan, Thomas

- private, Eighth Regiment, New Jersey Infantry, enlisted May 1862
- corporal, July 1862
- discharged, May 1865

DEFORREST, ISAAC

- private, Company K, Second New Jersey Regiment, enlisted May 1861
- discharged for disability February 1863

FOURATT, GEORGE E.

- private, Company F, Twenty-eighth New Jersey Regiment, enlisted July 1862
- discharged July 1863

FURLONG, JAMES

- private, New Jersey Volunteers, Company K, First Infantry, enlisted June 1861
- full corporal, September 1862
- wounded at Antietam Valley, September 1862
- transferred October 1862 into Battery A, First New Jersey Light Artillery
- discharged June 1864

FURLONG, WILLIAM

- private, Company F, Twenty-eighth New Jersey Regiment, enlisted August 1862
- discharged July 1863

HAMILTON, ALEXANDER, JR.

- second lieutenant, Company K, Nineteenth Indiana Regiment, enlisted April 1861
- discharged July 1861
- private, Company H, Nineteenth U.S. Infantry, First Battalion, enlisted November 1861
- provost guard, Army of the Potomac, May 1862
- discharged November 1964

HAMILTON, ALEXANDER, SR.

- private, Company D, Fifty-seventh Pennsylvania Volunteers, enlisted November 1861
- wounded, Fair Oaks, June 1862
- discharged with disability November 1862
- died January 1864

HAMILTON, JAMES W.

- corporal, Company F, Eleventh New Jersey Infantry Regiment, enlisted June 1862
- killed in action at Chancellorsville, Virginia, May 3, 1863

HAMILTON, JOHN P.

- private, Company K, First New Jersey Regiment, enlisted June 1861
- transferred October 1862 into Battery A, First New Jersey Light Artillery
- discharged June 1864

LEWIS, JOHN T.

- private, Company G, First New Jersey Infantry, enlisted August 1861
- transferred Company G, Fourth New Jersey Regiment
- discharged August 1864

MCGOVERN, PETER

- private, Company F, First New Jersey Regiment, enlisted May 1861
- discharged with disability January 1863

MOFFETT, BENJAMIN L.

- second lieutenant, Company F, First New Jersey Regiment, enlisted April 1863
- sergeant May 1862
- corporal May 1861
- killed in action at the Wilderness, Virginia, May 8, 1864

MYERS, JULIUS

- private, Company F, First New Jersey Infantry Regiment, enlisted June 1861
- discharged June 1864

SEVERANCE, MATTHEW S.

private, Company M, Sixteenth Georgia Infantry, enlisted August 1861
transferred Company B, Twenty-sixth Georgia Regiment, May 1862

SKILLMAN, DAVID

- private, Company G, First New Jersey Infantry Regiment, enlisted August 1861
- discharged August 1864

Stelle, George M.

- first lieutenant, Company I, Eighth New Jersey Volunteers, September 1861
- captain, Company F, Eighth New Jersey Regiment
- discharged October 1864

Stroud, William F.

- private, Company F, Twenty-eighth New Jersey Infantry, enlisted September 1862
- sergeant, March 1863
- discharged July 1863

Vroom, John

- private, Company A, First New Jersey Regiment, enlisted February 1862
- discharged June 1865

Wanser, Jarvis

- first sergeant, Company H, Fourteenth New Jersey Infantry Regiment, enlisted August 1862
- second lieutenant, Company F, May 1864
- first lieutenant, August 1864
- captain, Company B, December 1864
- discharged June 1865

Welsh, Michael

- private, Company F, First New Jersey Infantry Regiment, enlisted May 1861
- discharged June 1864

Bibliography

Aldrich, Nelson W., ed. *Wholesale Prices, Wages and Transportation*. Washington, D.C.: Government Printing Office, 1893.

Clayton, N. Woodford, ed. *History of Union and Middlesex Counties New Jersey with Illustrations.* Philadelphia, PA: Everts & Peck, J.B. Lippincott & Company, 1882.

Constable, George, ed. *Lee Takes Command: From Seven Days to Second Bull Run.* Alexandria, VA: Time-Life Books, 1984.

Eckhardt, Charles, and Robert MacAvoy. *Our Brothers Gone Before: An Inventory of Graves and Cenotaphs in New Jersey Cemeteries for Union and Confederate Civil War Soldiers, Sailors, Marines, Surgeons and Nurses*. Hightstown, NJ: Longstreet House, 2006.

Ellis, Edward S. *Twentieth Century History of the United States*. New York: R.S. Belcher Company, 1900.

Esposito, Vincent J., ed. *The West Point Atlas of American Wars.* Vol. 1, *1689–1900*. New York: Frederick A. Praeger Publishers, 1959.

Foner, Philip S. *Women and the American Labor Movement: From Colonial Times to the End of World War I.* New York: Free Press, 1979.

Frank, Lisa Tondrich, ed. *Women in the American Civil War*. Santa Barbara, CA: ABC-CLIO Inc., 2008.

Frassanito, William A. *Grant and Lee: The Virginia Campaigns, 1864–1865*. New York: Charles Scribner's Sons, 1983.

Gaffney, Dennis, and Peter Gaffney. *The Seven-Day Scholar: The Civil War, Exploring History One Week at a Time*. New York: Hyperion, 2011.

Gannon, Fred A. *A Short History of American Shoemaking*. Salem, MA: Newcomb & Gauss Printers, 1912.

Hall, Tony, ed. *Rebels and Yankees: The Commanders of the Civil War*. London: Salmander Books Ltd., 2001.

Hoisington, Daniel J. *Gettysburg and the Christian Commission*. Roseville, MN: Edinborough Press, 2002.

Holmes, Amy E. "Such Is the Price We Pay: American Widows and the Civil War Pension Systems." *Toward a Social History of the American Civil War: Exploratory Essays*. Cambridge, MA: Press Syndicate, 1990.

Jackson, Donald Dale, and the editors of Time Life Books. *Twenty Million Yankees: The Northern Home Front*. Morristown, NJ: Silver Burdett Company, 1985.

King, Janet. "Part III: The Surgical War." Vermont Civil War. http://vermontcivilwar.org/medic/medicine.

Kull, Irving S., ed. *New Jersey: A History*. Vol. 3. New York: American Historical Society Inc., 1930.

———. *New Jersey: A History*. Vol. 2. New York: American Historical Society Inc., 1930.

Marbaker, Thomas D. *History of the Eleventh New Jersey Volunteers*. Hightstown, NJ: Longstreet House, 2012.

Massey, Mary Elizabeth. *Bonnet Brigades: American Women and the Civil War*. New York: Alfred A. Knopf, 1966.

McCrosson, W. Rex. *A Short Summary of the History of the New Jersey Homes for Disabled Soldiers at Newark, Kearny and Vinland.* Trenton, NJ: NJDMAVA, 1954.

McPherson, James M. *Battle Cry of Freedom: The Civil War Era.* New York: Oxford University Press, Ballantine Books, 1988.

Methodism in New Brunswick, NJ, 1811–1961, and the Commemoration of the Union of the Methodist Churches. New Brunswick, NJ, 1961.

Regan, Timothy E. *Images of America: New Brunswick.* Charleston, SC: Arcadia Publishing, 1996.

Robinson, James I., Jr., ed. *Tenting Tonight: The Soldier's Life.* Morristown, NJ: Time-Life Books, 1984.

Scott, Robert N., comp. *The War of the Rebellion: The Official Records of the Union and Confederate Armies.* 128 vols. Washington, D.C.: U.S. Government Printing Office, 1882–1900.

Sears, Stephen W. *Chancellorsville.* New York: Houghton Mifflin, 1996.

———. *To the Gates of Richmond: The Peninsula Campaign.* New York: Houghton Mifflin, 1992.

Thomson, Ross. *The Path to Mechanized Shoe Production in the United States.* Chapel Hill: University of North Carolina Press, 2012.

VA History in Brief. Virginia pamphlet No. 80-97-2. Washington, D.C.: Virginia Office of Public Affairs, 1997.

Von Hoffman, Alexander W. "Origins of American Housing Reform." Joint Center for Housing Studies, Harvard University, August 1998.

Weeks, Joseph D., ed. *Report on the Statistics of Wages in Manufacturing Industries.* 1880 Census, vol. 20, 1884, Department of the Interior. Washington, D.C.: Government Printing Office, 1886.

Index

A

B

C

D

R

S

U

V

W

About the Author

Joanne Hamilton Rajoppi, a former journalist, is a history aficianado. Serving as a trustee of the Union County Historical Society, she currently chairs the county's Civil War Sesquicentennial Exhibit and is the author of several pamphlets and calendars detailing the history of the region. A lifelong resident of New Jersey, she loves the rich history of the area and its people. She serves as the county clerk of Union County and is a former mayor of her hometown.

Visit us at
www.historypress.net

....

This title is also available as an e-book

www.ingramcontent.com/pod-product-compliance
Lightning Source LLC
LaVergne TN
LVHW010944100826
845153LV00002B/137

* 9 7 8 1 5 4 0 2 2 2 2 0 6 *